New Directions for
Adult and Continuing
Education

Susan Imel
Jovita M. Ross-Gordon
COEDITORS-IN-CHIEF

Continuing Education in Colleges and Universities: Challenges and Opportunities

Ronald G. White
Frank R. DiSilvestro
EDITORS

Number 140 • Winter 2013
Jossey-Bass
San Francisco

CONTINUING EDUCATION IN COLLEGES AND UNIVERSITIES: CHALLENGES AND OPPORTUNITIES
Ronald G. White, Frank R. DiSilvestro (eds.)
New Directions for Adult and Continuing Education, no. 140
Susan Imel, Jovita M. Ross-Gordon, Coeditors-in-Chief

© 2013 Wiley Periodicals, Inc., A Wiley Company. All rights reserved. No part of this publication may be reproduced, stored in a retrieval system, or transmitted in any form or by any means, electronic, mechanical, photocopying, recording, scanning, or otherwise, except as permitted under Section 107 or 108 of the 1976 United States Copyright Act, without either the prior written permission of the Publisher or authorization through payment of the appropriate per-copy fee to the Copyright Clearance Center, 222 Rosewood Drive, Danvers, MA 01923, (978) 750-8400, fax (978) 646-8600. The copyright notice appearing at the bottom of the first page of an article in this journal indicates the copyright holder's consent that copies may be made for personal or internal use, or for personal or internal use of specific clients, on the condition that the copier pay for copying beyond that permitted by law. This consent does not extend to other kinds of copying, such as copying for distribution, for advertising or promotional purposes, for creating collective works, or for resale. Such permission requests and other permission inquiries should be addressed to the Permissions Department, c/o John Wiley & Sons, Inc., 111 River Street, Hoboken, NJ 07030; (201) 748-6011, fax (201) 748-6008, www.wiley.com/go/permissions.

Microfilm copies of issues and articles are available in 16mm and 35mm, as well as microfiche in 105mm, through University Microfilms Inc., 300 North Zeeb Road, Ann Arbor, Michigan 48106-1346.

NEW DIRECTIONS FOR ADULT AND CONTINUING EDUCATION (ISSN 1052-2891, electronic ISSN 1536-0717) is part of The Jossey-Bass Higher and Adult Education Series and is published quarterly by Wiley Subscription Services, Inc., A Wiley Company, at Jossey-Bass, One Montgomery Street, Suite 1200, San Francisco, CA 94104-4594. POSTMASTER: Send address changes to New Directions for Adult and Continuing Education, Jossey-Bass, One Montgomery Street, Suite 1200, San Francisco, CA 94104-4594.

New Directions for Adult and Continuing Education is indexed in CIJE: Current Index to Journals in Education (ERIC); Contents Pages in Education (T&F); ERIC Database (Education Resources Information Center); Higher Education Abstracts (Claremont Graduate University); and Sociological Abstracts (CSA/CIG).

INDIVIDUAL SUBSCRIPTION RATE (in USD): $89 per year US/Can/Mex, $113 rest of world; institutional subscription rate: $311 US, $351 Can/Mex, $385 rest of world. Single copy rate: $29. Electronic only—all regions: $89 individual, $311 institutional; Print & Electronic—US: $98 individual, $357 institutional; Print & Electronic—Canada/Mexico: $98 individual, $397 institutional; Print & Electronic—Rest of World: $122 individual, $431 institutional.

EDITORIAL CORRESPONDENCE should be sent to the Coeditors-in-Chief, Susan Imel, 3076 Woodbine Place, Columbus, Ohio 43202-1341, e-mail: imel.1@osu.edu; or Jovita M. Ross-Gordon, Southwest Texas State University, CLAS Dept., 601 University Drive, San Marcos, TX 78666.

Cover photograph by Jack Hollingsworth@Photodisc

www.josseybass.com

Contents

EDITORS' NOTES 1
Ronald G. White, Frank R. DiSilvestro

1. The Dynamic Flux of Continuing Higher Education: 7
Redefining the New Roles, Responsibilities, and Expectations
Lisa R. Braverman
The roles and expectations for continuing education programs and professionals are undergoing a period of rapid change.

2. Current Trends in Adult Degree Programs: How Public 17
Universities Respond to the Needs of Adult Learners
Angela Gast
With pressure to increase the number of adults with degrees, universities are responding with campus-based and online programs and specialized support services.

3. Partnerships with Academic Departments 27
Anthony M. English
This chapter offers practical suggestions and examples of successful collaborations between continuing education units and academic departments.

4. From Access to Excess: Changing Roles and Relationships 39
for Distance Education, Continuing Education, and Academic Departments in American Universities
Judy Copeland Ashcroft
This chapter describes the ways that continuing education units are utilizing distance and online learning in their programs as well as new developments in the use of technology.

5. Growing Importance of Prior Learning Assessment in the 51
Degree-Completion Toolkit
Rebecca Klein-Collins, Judith B. Wertheim
Although prior learning assessment has been around for several decades, recent developments, including the push to increase the number of adults with college degrees in the United States, have resulted in new developments in assessing learning outside of the classroom.

6. Trends and Considerations Affecting Noncredit Programs 61
Nelson C. Baker
This chapter focuses on considerations affecting the development of noncredit programs in a rapidly changing higher education landscape.

7. Role of the Community College in Economic Development 69
Rebecca A. Nickoli
This chapter discusses the innovative ways that community colleges are playing an increasing role in local and regional economic development.

8. Continuing Higher Education and Older Adults: A Growing 79
Challenge and Golden Opportunity
Frank R. DiSilvestro
This chapter focuses on the rapidly aging U.S. population and its impact on the role of continuing higher education.

9. Preparing Marketing for the Future: Strategic Marketing 89
Challenges for Continuing Education
James Fong
This chapter describes how societal needs and new developments in continuing education are reshaping the role of marketing and program promotion.

10. The Road Ahead: Challenges and Opportunities 101
Ronald G. White
This chapter summarizes the major issues and developments addressed in this volume and some of the challenges continuing higher education is likely to face in the coming years.

INDEX 107

Editors' Notes

Dramatic changes in society, the economy, and technology are altering higher education and, with it, continuing education schools and programs in colleges and universities. "Nontraditional" adult learners now outnumber traditional, full-time, residential college students, and the noncredit arena explodes with more program models, technologies, and audiences, all of which must respond to greater demands for fiscal accountability. As a result, continuing education (CE) programs seem to be at a critical juncture. Those that choose to continue business as usual might very well face extinction; however, those that anticipate and respond to these changes can provide critical leadership not only for their own programs but also play a major role in their institutions.

Due to the historical mission of their units as well as professional experience, CE staff members have the expertise to assume campuswide leadership roles in community outreach, economic development, internal and external partnerships, and distance education, all of which are now having greater impact on other campus departments. While CE units have always been at the nexus of campus and community, expectations and opportunities are increasing on a number of fronts. In this volume we explore some of these developments and their potential impact on CE units.

Historically, CE programs have not been especially prestigious in the university hierarchy. Baden (1999) stated that from the 1970s to the 1990s, CE units often were marginalized and their staff felt like second-class citizens on campuses. CE needs and priorities received less emphasis than those for students of traditional ages. Despite the fact that many CE units were generating substantial revenues for their institutions, their leaders seldom had much influence on institutional direction and resource allocation.

While we would all hope that this has changed in the 21st century, an increase in stature for CE units has been slow and uneven, even nonexistent in some institutions. Despite this, the past 20 years have been a period of significant transition for CE, according to Cervero (2001) who points to four trends: (1) more programs are being offered online; (2) there is increased collaboration among adult learning providers including universities and employers; (3) CE units are increasingly operated like businesses; and (4) CE is becoming a requirement for more and more professions.

Yankelovich (2005) believes that a number of trends will transform higher education in general; his predictions also include implications for CE practice. First, the longer life span (average of 47 in 1900 and nearly 90 in the current century) will disrupt the prevailing pattern of education, then work, replaced by greater integration of the two as well as alternate—or concurrent—periods of each. Longer periods of retirement will increase the demand for education for second careers as well as for personal enjoyment, providing new programming opportunities for CE.

There will also be greater pressure to understand different cultures and languages since businesses will be increasingly international in scope, and the risk of cultural isolation could undermine the global leadership of the United States (Yankelovich, 2005). Further, Yankelovich (2005) believes that the growing social and economic inequality in the United States will motivate workers to engage in continuous skills upgrading to remain competitive, and this will foster additional higher education–corporate partnerships.

The context for CE is also changing to incorporate skills and competencies for global interdependence, leadership, and innovation, according to Walshok (2012), who sees both challenges and opportunities for continuing education:

1. In the 1950s to the 1970s, the role of CE was often viewed as providing a second chance for adults; today, CE units are vital hubs of reeducation and training, especially for the millennials (those born after 1980), who realize that a bachelor's degree is not sufficient for career advancement, contributing to record growth in both credit and noncredit certificate programs.
2. To promote innovation, CE needs to assume an active role in local and regional economic development, by providing technical assistance, mentoring, and business incubators as well as career-focused courses.
3. CE units in research institutions must do more than provide access for adults to traditional curricula; they should also help individuals prepare for their next career stage by building skills and knowledge portfolios and providing advising throughout the life span to assist individuals as they transition in and out of educational experiences.
4. There will be more partnering with K–12 schools, community colleges, employers, and regional planning groups to develop the local workforce and have access to resources that the university does not possess.

Walshok (2012) believes that meeting these challenges will require CE professionals with the skills to network and integrate information across multiple fields of learning in order to develop programs that bridge the "world of ideas and the world of action" (p. 51). To accomplish this, she urges CE units to assume greater presence in the civic, cultural, and economic life of their communities.

Gratton (2011) argues that the modern university tends to function as an entity separated from the larger community with a primary focus on full-time students but that CE units can be the bridge for increased interaction with external communities. She describes ours as an age in which continuous learning is essential for career success and argues that working people need environments where they can network to develop relational and collaborative opportunities as well as the skills to interact with multiple local and global communities.

Kasworm (2012) underscores this need for community linkage and notes that higher education in general is being pressured into being more responsive to regional and statewide economic development. In addition, the need for more Americans to earn bachelor's degrees to remain competitive in the global marketplace will remain critical.

According to Schroeder (2013), universities will increasingly be called on to assess and interpret learning experiences that students have accumulated through online courses, careers, and personal learning networks in addition to traditional courses. He believes that to remain relevant, universities must rethink the traditional transcript to include competencies and understandings rather than course prefixes and titles. The college transcript of the future will describe learning activities that have been pursued both within and outside of the academy, in a classroom or online, some for credit and others not. This development will have special relevance for adult learners who often bring a wealth of experience to the classroom.

New York Times columnist and author Tom Friedman (2013a) believes that a global revolution is occurring in online education as a result of massive open online courses (MOOCs). MOOCs are noncredit, open enrollment, free courses currently offered by several prestigious schools, such as Harvard, MIT, and Stanford, where thousands can and do enroll in a single course. Although the large number of students results in little or no interaction with faculty, MOOCs can promote the interaction of people from different backgrounds and cultures, in addition to the content learned.

These courses do not ordinarily carry college credit, but there are ongoing discussions on ways to make these offerings creditworthy. Some providers are offering proctored exams and even certification for transfer credit through the American Council on Education (Lewin, 2013). The dramatic possible impact of this on adult degree programs expands on current means of transferring credits, earning credit for prior learning, and other modes of demonstrating competence (Peale, 2013).

Friedman (2013a) sees the possibility of students creating their own degrees with online courses selected from the best faculty in the world. Similarly, Peale (2013) describes this as the "unbundling" of degrees by which students will choose among online courses from multiple institutions, thus pursuing a degree "cobbled together on your laptop at home" (para. 1).

Mozilla's Open Badges project also recognizes that learning occurs in many ways and locations in addition to traditional higher education (Watters, 2011), yet much of it is not "counted." Badges are certificates that demonstrate competence and can be earned from sources other than formal higher education. These credentials could precipitate a shift from formal educational settings to other venues, such as the workplace and online sites, where teaching and learning can occur on a daily basis.

These badges represent what Friedman (2013b) describes as the transition from a focus on "time served" to "stuff learned" (para. 6), leading to a more competency-based educational system with less emphasis on where you learned something than what you learned. CE has a vital role to play in these new ways of certifying learning due to its role in linking campuses with the larger community and the economy.

Because CE programs vary so much among institutions, it was a challenge to select issues and developments to include in the current issue. Chapters in this issue highlight those issues and developments that seem to have wide application and relevance and are intended to provide useful information for both new and experienced CE professionals in higher education settings.

In Chapter 1, Lisa R. Braverman introduces this *New Directions* issue by describing how the roles and expectations for both continuing education programs and professionals are undergoing a period of rapid change.

Chapter 2, by Angela Gast, examines one of these changing expectations—that of increasing the number of adults with degrees; she describes some of the current trends in adult degree programs and related student services.

Partnerships, both internal and external, are increasingly being developed by CE units. In Chapter 3, Anthony M. English discusses the steps necessary for successful partnerships, as well as some of the pitfalls to avoid.

Judy Copeland Ashcroft addresses the evolution of online learning, including the recent emergence of MOOCs, as well as the changing roles of CE units in using technology to extend learning opportunities, in Chapter 4.

Prior learning assessment has been a mainstay of adult degree programs for some time, but new means of documenting learning outside the classroom are being developed. These areas are discussed by Rebecca Klein-Collins and Judith B. Wertheim in Chapter 5.

Noncredit programs are becoming more businesslike in operation, and there is a never-ending need to develop new offerings to respond to changing demographics as well as internal and external expectations. Nelson C. Baker explains these changes in Chapter 6.

Community colleges are increasingly seen as engines of economic development. Customized training for employers as well as innovative links with secondary schools and universities are being developed to provide more seamless career education and participation in local development activities. In Chapter 7, Rebecca A. Nickoli explores these trends and sample programs.

The growth of the older adult population, coupled with new advances in the study of learning, has resulted in new opportunities for CE programming. Frank R. DiSilvestro discusses the educational opportunities and challenges presented by this growing demographic in Chapter 8.

CE marketing departments are experiencing significant transformation as a result of new technologies, strategies, and customer media preferences. In Chapter 9, James Fong discusses these developments as well as their implications for CE marketing in the future.

In Chapter 10, Ronald G. White summarizes the issues and developments discussed in this volume and anticipates some of the challenges and opportunities that CE units in higher education will face in the years ahead.

Ronald G. White
Frank R. DiSilvestro
Editors

References

Baden, C. (1999). Reinventing continuing education. *Journal of Continuing Higher Education, 47*(3), 33–36.
Cervero, R. (2001). Continuing professional education in transition. *International Journal of Lifelong Education, 12*(1–2), 16–30.
Friedman, T. (2013a, January 26). Revolution hits the universities. *New York Times*. Retrieved from http://www.nytimes.com/2013/01/27/opinion/sunday/friedman-revolution-hits-the-universities.html
Friedman, T. (2013b, March 5). The professor's big stage. *New York Times*. Retrieved from http://www.nytimes.com/2013/03/06/opinion/friedman-the-professors-big-stage.html
Gratton, L. (2011). *The shift: The future of work is already here.* New York, NY: Collins.
Kasworm, C. (2012). U.S. adult higher education: One context of lifelong. *International Journal of Continuing Education and Lifelong Learning, 5*(1), 1–17.
Lewin, T. (2013, April 30). Colleges adapt online courses to ease burden. *New York Times*. Retrieved from http://www.nytimes.com/2013/04/30/education/colleges-adapt-online-courses-to-ease-burden.html
Peale, C. (2013, March 18). The university of the future? *Cincinnati Enquirer*. Retrieved from http://news.cincinnati.com/article/20130317/NEWS0102/303180041/IN-DEPTH-university-future
Schroeder, R. (2013). Disrupting the degree? Credentialing in 2023. *The EvoLLLution*. Retrieved from http://www.evolllution.com/opinions/disrupting-degree-credentialing-2023/
Walshok, M. (2012). Reinventing continuing higher education. *Continuing Higher Education Review, 76*, 38–53.
Watters, A. (2011, November 15). How will Mozilla's open badges project affect higher ed? *Inside Higher Education*. Retrieved from http://www.insidehighered.com/blogs/hack-higher-education/how-will-mozillas-open-badges-project-affect-higher-ed
Yankelovich, D. (2005, November 25). Ferment and change: Higher education in 2015. *Chronicle of Higher Education*, p. 6.

RONALD G. WHITE, *EdD, is adjunct associate professor of adult education at Indiana University, where he also served as executive director of continuing studies for the Bloomington campus.*

FRANK R. DISILVESTRO *is associate professor of adult education, program coordinator for the graduate program in adult education, and part-time associate professor of medical education at Indiana University.*

1

> Continuing higher education has undergone a significant transformation in recent years, illustrated by such innovations as MOOCs, globalization, strategic collaborations with government and industry, and increased entrepreneurship. As a result, continuing education (CE) units have experienced a fundamental shift in the way they conduct business in our field.

The Dynamic Flux of Continuing Higher Education: Redefining the New Roles, Responsibilities, and Expectations

Lisa R. Braverman

Introduction

Continuing education (CE) organizations have undergone historic transformations in recent years in both the roles that they perform and the audiences they serve. CE practice in the United States has had to accommodate the explosion in adult enrollments that has been occurring since the late 1980s (National Center for Education Statistics, 2009). During this time, according to adult enrollment expert Carol Aslanian, "career-oriented programs of study, convenient schedules and locations, and age-based services needed to be created or expanded to meet the academic and logistical needs of older learners" (Aslanian & Green Giles, 2011, p. 2). According to their research, in 2011, over 40% of all higher education enrollments consisted of students age 25 or older. In response to the dramatic rise in adult students on campuses across the nation, colleges shifted resources and personnel by expanding or creating substantial new departments and schools of continuing and adult education to cope with this growth. Aslanian's theory that adult students are most often involved in a life transition meant that campuses had to understand and serve these adults in increasingly supportive and flexible ways.

The general population possessed greater disposable income in the late 1990s to spend on self-enrichment and college study. By the early 2000s, world events and the dot-com bust forced a downward cycle in enrollments and revenue for most CE units, especially in noncredit, short course offerings. According to a report funded by the Sloan Consortium (Allen & Seaman,

2013), distance education enrollments, however, continued to climb, as did credit enrollments. Just as noncredit programs began to stabilize, the Great Recession of 2008 quickly drove down course enrollments in both credit and noncredit programs. Many out-of-work adults were forced to return to study at more affordable community colleges to meet the urgent need for additional career skills during this time (Mullin & Phillippe, 2009).

Better Business

The economic fluctuations since the 1990s also forced CE professionals to become better business practitioners. Professional development for continuing educators included more numerous financial management and budgeting workshops at the University Professional Continuing Education Association (UPCEA) national annual conferences from 2003 to 2007 than had been the case in prior years. The days of offering CE programs philanthropically without calculating their profitability became a thing of the past. From the early 2000s on, successful continuing educators were required to demonstrate entrepreneurial skills and greater fiscal accountability in order to keep their jobs in a more competitive, rapidly changing CE market. The upheavals in the nation's economic and social landscape characterizing this period greatly impacted higher education. Financially strapped as a result of diminishing state contributions, colleges increasingly required greater self-sufficiency and "stand-alone" status for their CE units, particularly following the Great Recession of 2008.

In order to achieve the necessary transformation from an academic to a business model, modern CE units became more streamlined, more centralized, and smaller. Few CE units today can boast a workforce of 100 employees or more as was once the case, except for premier private colleges and larger public universities. However, in recent years, even the smaller CE units have had to lay off employees or be retrenched altogether. During this time, colleges and universities displayed ambivalence about doing away with their CE units, but neither could they always afford to subsidize them. All of this put pressure on CE units nationwide to become leaner, nimbler and, especially, more innovative.

Major universities, such as Ohio State and the University of Maryland, downsized their CE units. The continuing studies unit at the University of Maryland, for example, was dismantled, and summer sessions operations were centralized under the provost's office. A campus within the State University of New York (SUNY) system that served over 15,000 students was also absorbed into the provost's office.

In all three cases, the functions associated with these units were abruptly incorporated into traditional academic areas or eliminated altogether, as campuses sought ways to reduce costs and control revenue at a time of sizable state budget reductions and declining enrollments. Campus leaders underestimated the rich opportunities that the economic downturn offered colleges and CE units. Faced with shrinking resources and insufficient relationships with the external community, many higher education executives focused too narrowly on cost containment, at the expense of strategic innovation and growth. Those campuses that managed to seize new opportunities emerged stronger and more profitable as a result of connections that they had forged at this time. The trend toward cost benefit analysis rather than innovation continues to be seen at some colleges, but the national agenda toward adult degree completion and career-ready education is, finally, counteracting this.

Innovation

In response to shifts in the nation's economy, continuing educators have had to embrace and lead the innovations in higher education. In 2011, the president of the University Continuing Professional Education Association launched a new project known as the New and Aspiring Leaders program that was designed to reignite innovation into the field by shaping the next generation of CE leaders. Similarly, the Association of Continuing Higher Education underscored entrepreneurship at its 2012 annual conference, titled "Collaboration and Partnership: Our Keys to the Future." Senior CE executives today debate and discuss the qualities needed for successful CE leadership and work to identify ways that CE membership associations might best address such issues at their annual conferences.

The following are critical areas of continuing higher education innovation:

1. CE units must be able to master all aspects of online education, including faculty development, educational technologies, online student needs, distance pedagogy, and outcomes assessment. Distance education is clearly the future, according to data from the Sloan Consortium, which is tracking the enormous surge in students taking classes online (Allen & Seaman, 2013).
2. Global education and international partnerships have been incorporated into the daily practice of most major CE units, as emerging nations increasingly seek out American universities for the purposes of student and faculty exchanges or to purchase education and skills training from the West.
3. In the wake of the 2008 recession, many CE units created new partnerships with municipal agencies, government offices, workforce investment boards, and the U.S. Department of Labor, entities that provided them with generous funding for skills training and retooling of retrenched workers to help stimulate the floundering national economy.

4. CE units nationally also offered skills building and consulting to corporations and firms to help improve the competitiveness of U.S. business and industry globally.
5. The transformation of the American population and its shifting demographics has demanded new knowledge, responsiveness, and creativity on the part of continuing educators in offering programs and curricula that successfully embrace the dramatic new diversity occurring in American society.

As mirrored in the titles of the individual networks—special interest groups that members may join—within the University Professional Continuing Education Association (n.d.), these five areas—distance education, international partnerships, government-sponsored workforce development, corporate partnerships and outreach, and programs that respond to a society in the midst of an extraordinary demographic transformation—are just some fields of practice that illustrate the newer, more innovative approaches being adopted by successful CE units.

Distance Education

As would be expected, technology drives the major innovations in the field of continuing higher education today. MOOCs—massive open online courses—and related developments have dominated higher education headlines. Innovations like MOOCs represent a trend toward democratizing higher education by providing access for the multitudes, rather than for a privileged few, at the same time that the basic mission of conventional higher education has come under fire. Articles appearing in such well-respected periodicals as the *Economist* debate the value American higher education as overpriced, outdated, and of questionable value to the nation's young adults ("Not What It Used to Be," 2012) and call into question higher education's basic value proposition.

In more conventional online education programs, colleges and universities continue building scalable models that infuse technology into classroom teaching to improve enrollments and recruit new classes of adult and Gen X students. According to the Sloan Consortium in 2008, distance education grew at a rate that was 10 times that of higher education annually (Allen & Seaman, 2008, p. 5). The net result of these dramatic shifts now require that continuing educators who manage online education for their campuses remain current and capable of leading innovative new models of technologically infused education while identifying paradigms for change at their home institutions.

Although technology currently dominates education innovation and changes the way we teach and learn, it has also fundamentally changed the way continuing higher education is marketed. Research conducted by enrollment management firms such as Stamats Higher Education Marketing (2007) and others indicate that the primary method for seeking information on higher education is the Internet. In sharp contrast to Web navigation just four or five years ago, social media sites, such as Facebook, LinkedIn, and Twitter, provide electronic forums where students can speak to one another or with peers, offering opinions, sharing practices and photos, and providing uncensored opinions about programs and professors that are immediately accessed and virally distributed. As a result, continuing educators have begun adding social media marketers to their staffing configurations and training them in digital media and marketing to ensure that their program Web pages are lively and enticing to prospective learners. Most major programs at colleges and universities desiring to remain viable have pages on Facebook and Twitter. Social media marketing skills are critical for continuing educators to remain competitive in today's fast-moving, digitally oriented education marketplace.

International Partnerships

In his landmark book about international higher education expansion entitled *The Great Brain Race: How Global Universities Are Reshaping the World,* author Ben Wildavsky (2010) states that "for a burgeoning number of universities, national boundaries have become irrelevant ... the same forces of globalization that have shaken up almost every sector of the economy have greatly intensified competition and mobility in higher education" (p. 3). He goes on to say that "western universities are acting more like businesses—moving closer to their customers by establishing satellite campuses in Asia and the Middle East, and teaming up with overseas universities to forge strategic alliances that offer scholarly and marketing advantages to both sides" (p. 4).

Opportunities in international education have never been so plentiful or so rewarding for institutions of higher education as they are today. Prestigious colleges and universities compete for the best students globally, opening branch campuses in far-flung locations such as Bangalore, Qatar, and China if it means they can recruit new audiences for their degree programs and derive benefit from today's global higher education expansion revolution. Both faculty and classrooms are becoming more portable and internationalized in such programs as Tisch Asia, where New York University (NYU) incorporated Singaporean culture into its arts and film education at its Singapore campus, or Abu Dhabi, where, as noted on its Web site, it has established itself as "One Global University ... with a fully integrated liberal arts and science college" (New York University, n.d.). In a 2013 speech, Carnegie Mellon's president, Subra Suresh, noted that as a university with campuses on five continents, the "sun never sets on Carnegie Mellon" (Carnegie Mellon University, 2013, para. 3).

Despite recent objections to international expansion raised by faculty at universities such as Yale and NYU who are concerned that their institutions may not be able to maintain academic quality abroad, efforts continue to create international educational "hubs," or global geographical regions that are viable destinations for foreign universities to build campuses and recruit students. Universities are increasingly likely to enter into creative partnerships such as that between Johns Hopkins University and Perdana University in Malaysia. Together, the two plan to attract local and foreign students, develop the skills of people who will remain in the country, and build impressive research infrastructures (Jaschik, 2013).

As with other new practices and innovations in higher education, international education partnerships often were initiated by creative CE units and their leaders. Broad new revenue-generating opportunities increased for both public and private universities that delivered noncredit training and consulting work abroad in the BRIC (Brazil, Russia, India, and China) nations after 2008, when U.S. businesses, hobbled by the economy, could not afford to undertake new corporate training and education contracts, as evidenced by this writer's experience. The developing world, which had not suffered so much as the West, continued to exhibit enthusiasm for entering into education and training partnerships with American universities. As a result, colleges could realize a high premium for programs that transferred critical skills to these countries and their workforces.

Workforce Education and Training

Partnerships with local and municipal government agencies and workforce entities now constitute a large part of continuing higher education practice. The destructive effects of the recession on the nation's economy and resulting loss of jobs at rates not witnessed since the Great Depression resulted in the federal government's reinvestment of trillions of dollars into the economy, including $3.45 billion of funding earmarked specifically for job training and retooling in the American Recovery and Reinvestment Act of 2009 (ARRA). Funds provided by ARRA, the National Emergency Grant for those employees who lost jobs in the finance sector, and Trade Adjustment Assistance Community College and Career Training (TAACCCT) grants to the nation's community colleges in 2011 were just some of the programs designed to assist displaced workers by retraining them for new jobs. Continuing educators rose to the occasion, creating partnerships with government, Workforce Investment Boards (WIBs), Department of Labor offices, and local employers to lead the national response to worker retraining. Programs were created and important new linkages were forged between universities and the government sector. As a result of this effort, millions of workers attended college programs designed to retrain and build skills that would serve them in the new economy—an economy that, as experts warned, would be far more knowledge-based and have many fewer lower-skilled jobs. These municipal and federal partnerships required skilled expertise of continuing educators and drove innovation and change in their practice (California State University Office of Extended and Continuing Education, n.d.).

Corporate Education and Outreach

Corporate education and outreach through which a university creates vital connections to business and industry is yet another specialty that continuing educators have increasingly dominated in recent years. Private industry began reporting problems as it outsourced skills building to private training firms that delivered sophisticated staff development programs but left employees with no more than a scant recollection of what had been learned. As a result, colleges and universities began attracting more companies as clients of their CE units. As continuing educators grew more capable, interacting with businesses in ways that increasingly resonated with their clients—for example, offering just-in-time training, behaving more as vendors, accommodating client requests with greater speed and efficiency—partnerships between university and industry emerged. SUNY Farmingdale State College (2006) generated over $1 million in revenue between 2004 and 2005 from such corporate education partnerships and added many new corporate chief executive officers to its College Foundation. Revenue streamed in, joint programs were funded by partner firms, and benefits flowed in both directions. Colleges provided not only customized training programs but also other benefits, such as student interns, new graduates for hire, and expert faculty consulting services. Companies, in turn, paid their fees easily, became actively involved as board members, and provided generous, much-needed funding gifts that refurbished classrooms, restored buildings, and constructed new science and nursing labs. As the private industry and education sectors began to speak one another's language more as intertwined links in the supply chain of regional economic development, continuing educators led the way in developing these partnerships (Braverman, 2005).

Demographic Shifts

Shifting demographics is a fifth area in which continuing educators have applied their considerable ingenuity. Never before has American society seen such a diverse array of immigrants from such a wide variety of nations. As the world indeed grows increasingly flat, pointed out by best-selling author Thomas Friedman (2007), our society is growing more multicultural than ever before. In the suburban schools on Long Island, it is not uncommon for ethnic monitories to comprise up to 50% of a class, with children who speak Farsi, Spanish, Filipino, Hindi, and Mandarin all in one classroom. In a presentation at the UPCEA 2006 conference, Robert Lapiner, the former dean of extension at the University of California Los Angeles, said that for the first time in his city, whites did not constitute a majority of the population.

The influx of new immigrants and subsequent rise in the percentages of ethnic minorities that comprise our national fabric, coupled with the aging of the population, are creating one of the largest demographic shifts ever seen in American society. At a March 2012 conference on distance education at Long Island University, Carol Aslanian stated that by 2025, there will be more minorities attending classes on American colleges and university campuses than white students. The curricula that will be needed to meet the distinct needs of these diverse future student populations will challenge higher education leaders and put pressure on them to develop and deliver programs that span national differences, incorporate multicultural ideologies, teach inclusion, and address the needs of older Americans as the largest portion of American population—the baby boomer generation—ages. CE practitioners will need to rise to new levels of creativity and responsiveness. The magic bag of the continuing educator must continue to conjure up new responses in the form of future-focused curricula that are available online and via mobile devices in order to stay apace, add value, solve the compelling problems of our world, and provide gainful employment for a brand-new age of diverse Americans.

Conclusion

Doing more with less—and doing so to creatively and effectively drive the bottom line—characterizes the circumstances found in most CE units today. As a new knowledge economy emerges and the country is now faced with tens of millions of adults without bachelor's degrees, CE units are once again adding significant value on college campuses by providing increased access, adult-centric practices, career-ready programs, and support services for older learners who seek degrees and self-advancement that will, in turn, help restore competitiveness and productivity to the nation's economy.

Despite the economic fluctuations of the recent past, enrollment by students age 25 and older is predicted to continue to grow on campuses nationally for the foreseeable future. Through at least 2020, it is estimated that adult enrollments will increase at a higher rate than traditional-age enrollments (National Center for Education Statistics, 2011). Campuses and their leaders, once again, are calling on the expertise and resourcefulness of their adult and CE units to service this growth.

The ever-sweeping pendulum that characterizes continuing education is once again swinging back the other way, restoring the value of continuing higher education on today's campuses.

References

Allen, I. E., & Seaman, J. (2008). *Staying the course: Online education in the United States.* Wellesley, MA: SLOAN-C/Babson Survey Research Group. Retrieved from http://sloanconsortium.org/publications/survey/staying_course

Allen, I. E., & Seaman, J. (2013). *Changing course: Ten years of tracking online education in the United States.* Retrieved from http://www.onlinelearningsurvey.com/reports/changingcourse.pdf

American Recovery and Reinvestment Act of 2009. H.R. 1, 111th Cong., 1st Sess. (2009).

Aslanian, C., & Green Giles, N. (2011). *Hindsight foresight: Understanding adult learning trends to predict future opportunities.* Hoboken, NJ: Education Dynamics Market Research and Advisory Services.

Braverman, L. R. (2005). An innovative approach to extension and outreach in corporate education. *Journal of Continuing Higher Education, 53*(3), 28–31.

California State University Office of Extended and Continuing Education. (n.d.). *Working for California: The CSU and workforce development.* Retrieved from http://www.calstate.edu/extension/partnerships/documents/workforce_brochure.pdf

Carnegie Mellon University. (2013). *CMU welcomes President-Elect Dr. Subra Suresh.* Retrieved from http://www.cmu.edu/homepage/society/2013/winter/cmu-welcomes-president-elect.shtml

Friedman, T. (2007). *The world is flat.* New York, NY: Picador.

Jaschik, S. (2013, March 6). Classifying "education hubs." *Inside Higher Ed.* Retrieved from http://www.insidehighered.com/news/2013/03/06/scholars-discuss-how-define-and-evaluate-education-hubs

Mullin, C. M., & Phillippe, K. (2009). *Community college enrollment surge.* Washington, DC: American Association of Community Colleges. Retrieved from http://www.aacc.nche.edu/Publications/Briefs/Documents/enrollmentsurge_12172009.pdf

National Center for Education Statistics. (2009). *Digest of education statistics. Table 199, Total fall enrollment in degree-granting institutions, by sex, age, and attendance status: Selected years, 1970 through 2019.* Washington, DC: U.S. Department of Education, Institute of Education Science, National Center for Education Statistics. Retrieved from http://nces.ed.gov/programs/digest/d10/tables/dt10_199.asp

National Center for Education Statistics. (2011). *Projections of education statistics to 2020.* Retrieved from http://nces.ed.gov/pubsearch/pubsinfo.asp?pubid=2011026

New York University. (n.d.). *New York University, Abu Dhabi.* Retrieved from http://nyuad.nyu.edu/about.html

Not what it used to be. (2012, December 1). *Economist, 405*(8813), 29–30.

Stamats Higher Education Marketing. (2007, May 7). *FIT market research: Branding, image and strategic recruitment.* Special Report made by Stamats Higher Education Marketing to FIT Board of Trustees. Cedar Rapids, IA: Author.

SUNY Farmingdale State College. (2006). *Foundation member list.* Farmingdale, NY: Author.

University Professional Continuing Education Association. (n.d.). *Join a formal network in your area of practice.* Retrieved from http://upcea.edu/content.asp?pl=20&contentid=20

Wildavsky, B. (2010). *The great brain race: How global universities are reshaping the world.* Princeton, NJ: Princeton University Press.

LISA R. BRAVERMAN *is associate provost for adult programs and outreach at Long Island University, has been elected to the board of both the Association for Continuing Higher Education and the University Professional Continuing Education Association, and holds a PhD in foreign languages and international education from New York University.*

Although many adult students turn to online degree programs due to their flexibility and convenience, a majority of prospective adult learners prefer to take classes on traditional brick-and-mortar campuses. This chapter examines how public research universities create pathways to degree attainment and boost degree completion rates among adult students.

Current Trends in Adult Degree Programs: How Public Universities Respond to the Needs of Adult Learners

Angela Gast

Great attention is being placed on degree attainment within higher education and on the need to significantly boost the number of adults in the United States with some type of college credential. The rationale behind this drive is that a more highly educated society will lead to greater economic impacts—for both the individual and the society (Western Interstate Commission for Higher Education [WICHE], 2012). Initiatives to support this effort can be found at the national, state, and local levels, with President Obama, the Lumina Foundation, and many others leading this charge. For example, President Obama, through his Goal 2020, has called for reforms in the higher education system so that, by 2020, the United States once again leads the world in the proportion of college graduates (U.S. Department of Education, 2011). To achieve this goal, the U.S. Department of Education estimates that at least 8 million additional adults will need to return to college and earn associate and bachelor's degrees by the year 2020.

Although degree attainment rates in the United States have been relatively stagnant over the past decade, nearly every other industrialized nation has seen drastic increases in the number of adults holding college degrees (Kelly, 2010). According to the Lumina Foundation, a private organization focusing on increasing college degree completion rates in the United States, approximately 39% of adults in America hold a two- or four-year college degree. Through its Goal 2025 initiative, the Lumina Foundation seeks to raise that percentage to 60% by the year 2025, with the understanding that the nation will fall short of that goal if we focus only on traditional-age students (Lumina Foundation, 2012).

This chapter examines current trends in adult degree programs and services that aim to increase degree completion rates among adult students, with a specific focus on public research institutions, where, unlike many community colleges and for-profit institutions, adult education sometimes is located on the periphery of the institution's mission. Perceived barriers to higher education and degree completion among adult students also are discussed, and the efforts of public research universities to reduce or even eliminate these barriers and boost degree completion rates among this growing student population are examined.

Enrollment Trends Among Adult Students

According to the National Center for Education Statistics, enrollment levels among adult students have been consistently on the rise for the past 30 years, with recent figures indicating that adult students account for 40% of total postsecondary enrollment. The greatest increase in postsecondary enrollment from 2009 to 2020 is projected to be among students who are 25 and older. Those students who are between the ages of 25 to 34 years old have the highest projected increase of 21%, whereas traditional-age students (between 18 and 24) are projected to increase by only 9% (Hussar & Bailey, 2011).

What factors are influencing this growing enrollment trend among adult students? According to Kohl (2010), several factors are encouraging adults to return to the classroom: the need for updated skills to compete in a knowledge-based economy, a change in demographics due to immigration and higher retirement ages, technological advances bringing the classroom to the student, and a globalization of the higher education system. Most recently, online and for-profit institutions have been a primary beneficiary of this growing enrollment trend among adult learners. However, the consulting firm Eduventures found that only 38% of prospective adult students surveyed stated they would prefer to study fully or mostly online. Thus, the majority of prospective adult students would rather enroll in a traditional, on-campus degree program to meet their career and personal goals (Fain, 2012b).

Perceived Barriers

Many prospective adult students are facing barriers in returning to college, as evidenced by a survey that found fewer than 5% of adults interested in attending college actually enrolled in a given year (Fain, 2012b). Time and finances are cited as the most common barriers faced by adult students. A recent higher education marketing report found that only two-thirds of the colleges in a national poll reported targeting marketing efforts to adult learners, suggesting that a lack of information may be a third factor for why so many adults who would like to return to school are not following through and enrolling (Noel-Levitz, 2011).

Prospective adult students are dissuaded by tuition costs and time constraints. And while online degree programs partially address these problems, they do not always offer enough of a perceived value to attract this potential adult student market. In order for public research universities to attract this student market, they must address barriers of time, finances, and perceived value. Once recruited, adult students must be provided with specialized support services and have access to staff who recognize their unique needs and busy lifestyles. Adult students who indicate high levels of satisfaction with academic factors and campus support are more likely to demonstrate higher degree completion rates, lower loan default rates, and higher alumni giving (Noel-Levitz, 2011).

Response of Public Universities

Public universities are increasingly prominent in the field of online education and offer adult learners a variety of online options for degree completion.

Online Degree Programs. By offering degree programs that can be completed partially or entirely online, institutions help to reduce the barriers of time and finances. Many online degree programs have been offered by for-profit colleges, institutions that have come under heavy criticism lately due to aggressive recruiting tactics and high student loan debt (Stratford, 2012). Enrollment in for-profit degree programs has seen steep declines, although some say this is simply the right-sizing of an industry that experienced dramatic growth during an economic recession (Wolfgang, 2012).

Public research universities have also entered the online degree market, combining convenience and flexibility with highly recognized and valued reputations. For example, the research institutions of the Committee on Institutional Cooperation (n.d.) all offer some form of online education. Many of these institutions have begun to market a virtual campus, pooling the online and distance education resources of their flagship and satellite campuses and assembling them into one convenient online location. This portal of online resources allows prospective adult learners to easily explore online course and degree options without having to gather information from each individual campus. Examples of virtual campuses can be seen in the University of Wisconsin's e-Campus, the University of Nebraska Online, and IU Online, a recently launched point of access to all of Indiana University's online course and degree program offerings.

Hybrid Degree Programs. An alternative to offering a program entirely online that is gaining momentum is the hybrid degree program, where requirements are satisfied through both on-campus and online coursework. Often, admission into these bachelor's degree programs requires previous completion of at least 60 credit hours, which can be done through regional campuses or the local community college system. The remainder of the requirements can then be completed through online coursework offered by the degree-granting institution. The University of South Carolina (USC) will offer this type of degree completion program through its new Palmetto College, which began in fall 2013. Students interested in earning a bachelor's degree from USC who have already earned at least 60 credit hours from one of the system's regional campuses will now have the option of completing a bachelor's degree in a number of fields by taking classes entirely online (Mogilyanskaya, 2012). Further examples can be found at the University of Nebraska and Kansas State University, both of which offer online bachelor's degree completion programs for students with previously earned college credit.

Universities are recognizing that the line between the traditional-age student and the adult student is becoming blurred and that the flexibility of online learning is in high demand by both populations. Adult degree programs are not necessarily going to fade away as a result, especially in light of the increasing enrollments. However, these degree programs may be adapted and rebranded to incorporate all students with similar learning preferences and degree completion goals, thus making them more of a mainstream mission of the university than ever before.

Massive Open Online Courses. There are also rapid developments in the field of massive open online courses (MOOCs) with powerful backing by elite institutions and leaders in educational innovation. MOOCs are free online courses that are available to anyone with a computer and Internet access. Currently, these courses do not carry college credit; however, that may soon change. The American Council on Education (ACE), a higher education association that evaluates noncollegiate programs and provides academic credit recommendations to colleges and universities, is considering issues related to MOOCs, including the possibility of MOOCs carrying college credit and their potential impact on degree completion (Marklein, 2012).

Many elite higher education institutions, such as the Massachusetts Institute of Technology and Harvard University, have already embraced this method of teaching and learning, and many others have followed. The industry has a long way to go, though, before MOOCs gain mass acceptance. Many schools are waiting for more evidence of quality and value before aligning with MOOC providers (Marklein, 2012). This is exactly what the Bill & Melinda Gates Foundation (2012) is seeking to provide—a greater understanding of effective implementation and the potential impact of MOOCs. The foundation has awarded more than $3 million in grants to various organizations and institutions, such as Duke University and Michigan State University, both of which will be developing introductory and remedial-level MOOCs.

Issue of Transfer Credits

Students who, at some point in their education, transfer their credits from one institution to another end up taking an average of 10 additional credits to complete their degree compared to those students who do not transfer between institutions (WICHE, 2012). This adds up to more time and money that adult students, who are likely to have experienced at least one transfer, are forced to spend earning their degree. Finding ways that reduce or offset the loss of credit hours, and therefore speed up the time to degree completion, will help eliminate the barriers of time and money among adult students.

Partnerships. Partnerships between community colleges and universities are one way to address the loss of credit hours. For example, the Iowa Admissions Partnership Program allows students currently enrolled in a community college to receive specialized services by Iowa State University (n.d.), including transfer advising, on-campus housing, and guaranteed admission, if certain requirements are met. Similarly, Kansas State University (KSU, n.d.) offers a 2 + 2 partnership between itself and local and regional community and technical colleges. With this partnership, students can first earn an associate's degree from a local community or technical college and then move into an online bachelor's degree offered by KSU. These types of partnerships enable students to access the information and support they need in order to complete a successful transfer from a community college to a public research university, minimizing credit hour loss and maximizing the use of available resources at both institutions.

Online Resources. Universities can also ease the burden of transferring credits by providing online resources for evaluating transferability prior to applying for admission. In many cases, adult students who are weighing their options for returning to school must apply for admission to a school before knowing how many transfer credits will be accepted. To remedy this problem, students could be provided with the tools needed to make informed choices about the most efficient path to degree completion prior to admission. The Grad TX (n.d.) consortium is an example of multiple state universities coming together to create a single online resource for potential returning adult students. The online transfer tool allows users to enter their previously earned coursework and determine how their credits would count toward an online bachelor's degree at each of the participating universities. This kind of convenience is exactly what is needed in order to get adults, who are knowledgeable consumers, back to college and earning their degree without a loss of time or money.

Prior Learning Assessments

Adult learners are likely to have attended more than one college or university during the course of their education. Due to institutional policies regarding the acceptance of transfer credits, adults may lose some of their previously earned credits when transferring to a new institution. One possible offset to this loss of credit hours would be to earn credit for prior learning. Adults returning to the classroom often do so with a great deal of life experience, which in some cases may be deemed equivalent to college-level learning. The Council for Adult and Experiential Learning (CAEL; 2010) found that adult students who earned prior learning assessment (PLA) credits were two and a half times more likely to persist to graduation than those adult students who did not earn PLAs. PLAs, which are discussed in greater detail in Chapter 5, are defined as any of the following: standardized tests such as the College Level Examination

Program (CLEP) or DANTES Subject Standardized Tests (DSST), ACE-evaluated noncollegiate programs, institutionally evaluated training programs or challenge exams, or learning portfolio assessments. Of the 48 institutions surveyed by CAEL, 84% offered at least 4 of these PLA methods.

It is common for universities to accept standardized test credits and ACE-recommended credits. Learning portfolios, however, are not so widely accepted among public research institutions. The issue pertains to quality control and standardization of recommendations. CAEL (2012) has launched an initiative to address this through its Learning Counts program. Students would have the opportunity to earn ACE-recommended credits through a CAEL-certified faculty member portfolio review process. Learning portfolios still have a long way to go before attaining widespread acceptance. However, with the efforts of CAEL, both in researching the impact of learning portfolios on degree completion rates and by offering a standardized review process, the field of prior learning assessments is likely to see continued growth and innovation. The University of Wisconsin System, for example, has set a goal to double the number of students earning credit through PLA and has awarded grants to individual campuses seeking to broaden the scope of PLA programs (WICHE, 2012).

Adult Student Support Services

Services designed for special segments of the student population, such as military veterans, students with learning disabilities, or first-generation college students, are common on a college campus. Staff members are trained to work with the unique needs of each population, and programming is designed to support the college experience. Adult students can also benefit from these kinds of services.

Case for Specialized Services. Public research universities that seek to increase adult student access must evaluate the effectiveness of their services for older students. Adults lead busy lives and are not always able to seek help during normal business hours; nor are they always comfortable with seeking support services online. Tailoring services to accommodate the unique needs of adult students through both online and in-person experiences will enable universities to better support and retain students through to graduation.

A 2011 study (Wyatt, 2011) found that nontraditional students were less likely than their younger counterparts to engage in extracurricular activities on campus. However, they were more likely to engage in the classroom, through participation, interaction with faculty members, and arriving to class prepared. This study indicated that the unique needs of adult students require staff and faculty members to consider their time constraints if they are to be successful in their college careers. In return, adult learners have much to offer to the classroom learning experience through their preparation, participation, and wealth of life experiences.

This same study found that support programs designed specifically for adult students are more likely to attract participation than those that are open to students of all ages. Although adult students are less likely to be engaged in college extracurricular activities, they would be more likely to join a student organization dedicated to adult students.

Best Practices. Several examples of support services designed specifically for the adult student can be found in public research universities. The University of Wisconsin–Madison's Adult Career and Special Student Services office offers financial assistance and services such as workshops and academic advising specifically for adult students. It also has created a student group solely for returning adult students on campus, providing opportunities for social support and academic engagement (http://continuingstudies.wisc.edu/advising/).

Penn State offers a Web site that helps current and prospective adult students throughout Pennsylvania navigate the admissions process, online and on-campus degree options, and the various support services available. In addition to the vast online resource library found on the Web site, adult student advocates are located on each campus to serve as the primary contact for adult students. These advocates can connect students to campus resources and help with adult-specific issues, such as earning credits for prior learning experiences (http://www.outreach.psu.edu/adult-learners).

Another example is Indiana University–Bloomington's (n.d.) Adult Student Resources, which offers financial, academic, and social support services for returning adult students. Included among the online and in-person offerings is a peer tutoring program where current adult students, with expertise in either math or technology, work as tutors and provide assistance at no charge to their peers. In addition to face-to-face tutoring, an online library of video tutorials has been created in order to better serve students who do not have time to meet with a tutor.

All of these examples highlight practices found within public research institutions that demonstrate an understanding of the unique needs of both prospective and current adult students. They have been designed in ways that reduce or eliminate the barriers of time, money, and information so that adult students can more easily return to school and successfully complete their educational goals.

Moving Forward. Public research institutions will need to examine the services they currently offer and be willing to make necessary changes in order to accommodate the needs of adult students. Wyatt (2011) states that in addition to a basic orientation to the campus and university policy, adult students also require that faculty and staff members treat them as adults and understand their unique time constraints in order to be successful in their academic career. Specific recommendations for improving adult student engagement on campus include: peer tutoring labs and services specifically for students aged 25 and above, counselors and advisors who understand adult student issues, events that would attract adult students with their families, and communication strategies for reaching this student population and informing them of available opportunities (Wyatt, 2011).

Future Considerations

Adult student enrollment is likely to continue to grow and at a faster pace than among traditional-age students. As more initiatives are developed at national, state, and local levels, more doors will be opened for adult students to return to college. It will be up to individual institutions to decide how best to market their programs, foster a supportive environment, and prepare adult students for the workforce. One key question is how each institution will differentiate its product. When prospective adult students research their options for earning a degree, how will they make their decision of when and where to enroll? Affordability, best use of previously earned credits, an alignment with career goals, and adult student–friendly services will be likely considerations. Public universities will need to make their brand and the value of their degree known to prospective adult students and create clear pathways to degree attainment in order to attract and retain this growing student population and meet our nation's educational goals.

A key challenge will be to track adult student retention and degree completion data. Currently, 77% of institutions do not track these data for their adult student populations (Fain, 2012a). However, work is under way by the Western Association of Schools and Colleges to create templates for tracking adult student data that can be used to collect and compare retention and degree completion rates at the institutional level (Fain, 2012a). Once these benchmarks have been established, the effectiveness of adult degree completion initiatives can be assessed more accurately. This assessment also will give the institution an opportunity to identify gaps in services and develop enhanced programming to recruit and retain adult learners.

References

Bill & Melinda Gates Foundation. (2012). *Massive open online courses (MOOCs)*. Retrieved from http://www.gatesfoundation.org/postsecondaryeducation/Pages/massive-open-online-courses.aspx

Committee on Institutional Cooperation. (n.d.). *About CIC*. Retrieved from http://www.cic.net/about-cic

Council for Adult and Experiential Learning (CAEL). (2010). *Fueling the race to postsecondary success*. Chicago, IL: Klein-Collins.

Council for Adult and Experiential Learning (CAEL). (2012). *Learning counts*. Retrieved from http://www.learningcounts.org

Fain, P. (2012a, July 11). Accreditor will require colleges to stop ignoring adult student retention. *Inside Higher Ed*. Retrieved from http://www.insidehighered.com/news/2012/07/11/accreditor-will-require-colleges-stop-ignoring-adult-student-retention

Fain, P. (2012b, September, 19). *Mature market for online education*. Retrieved from http://newsle.com/article/0/46901097/

Grad TX. (n.d.). *About Grad TX*. Retrieved from http://gradtx.org/about

Hussar, W. J., & Bailey, T. M. (2011). *Projections of education statistics to 2020* (NCES 2011–026). Washington, DC: U.S. Department of Education, National Center for Education Statistics.

Indiana University–Bloomington. (n.d.). *Adult student resources*. Retrieved from http://asr.iub.edu/

Iowa State University. (n.d.). *Admissions partnership program.* Retrieved from http://www.admissions.iastate.edu/partnership

Kansas State University. (n.d.). *2 + 2 partnerships.* Retrieved from http://www.dce.k-state.edu/affiliations/2+2

Kelly, P. J. (2010). *Closing the college attainment gap between the U.S. and most educated countries, and the contributions to be made by the states.* Boulder, CO: National Center for Higher Education Management Systems.

Kohl, K. J. (2010). Coping with change and fostering innovation: An agenda for professional and continuing education. *Continuing Higher Education Review, 74,* 9–21.

Lumina Foundation. (2012). *A stronger nation through higher education.* Retrieved from http://www.luminafoundation.org/publications/A_Stronger_Nation-2012.pdf

Marklein, M. B. (2012, November 18). Online-education trend expands. *USA Today.* Retrieved from http://www.usatoday.com/story/news/nation/2012/11/18/more-on-board-with-online-education-trend-of-moocs/1713079/

Mogilyanskaya, A. (2012, September 23). U. of South Carolina crafts an online degree that students can afford. *Chronicle of Higher Education.* Retrieved from http://chronicle.com/article/U-of-South-Carolina-Crafts-an/134566/?cid=at&utm_source=at&utm_medium=en

Noel-Levitz. (2011). *2011 marketing and student recruitment practices at four-year and two-year institutions.* Retrieved from https://www.noellevitz.com/documents/shared/Papers_and_Research/2011/2011MARKETINGRECRUITINGPRACTICES.pdf

Stratford, M. (2012, July 30). Senate report paints a damning portrait of for-profit higher education. *Chronicle of Higher Education.* Retrieved from http://chronicle.com/article/A-Damning-Portrait-of/133253/

U.S. Department of Education. (2011). *Meeting the nation's 2020 goal: State targets for increasing the number and percentage of college graduates with degrees.* Retrieved from http://www.whitehouse.gov/sites/default/files/completion_state_by_state.pdf

Western Interstate Commission for Higher Education (WICHE). (2012). *Strategies for success: Promising ideas in adult college completion.* Boulder, CO: Lane.

Wolfgang, B. (2012, October 18). Once havens for jobless, for-profit colleges now face own downsizing. *Washington Times.* Retrieved from http://www.washingtontimes.com/news/2012/oct/18/once-havens-for-jobless-for-profit-colleges-now-fa/?page=all

Wyatt, L. G. (2011). Nontraditional student engagement: Increasing adult student success and retention. *Journal of Continuing Higher Education, 59,* 10–20.

ANGELA GAST, MS, is the director of adult student resources at Indiana University–Bloomington, where she has also directed the university's adult degree program and served as an academic advisor.

This chapter describes how professional and continuing higher education units can develop and sustain successful partnerships with academic departments in order to deliver educational programs effectively to students.

Partnerships with Academic Departments

Anthony M. English

At its heart, higher education is a cooperative endeavor. Students, professors, staff, and members of the community work together to create environments in which people learn, grow, discover their talents, and draw on reservoirs of accumulated knowledge in order to improve society and themselves. Professional and continuing education (CE) units play an important role in this educational process by extending the resources of a college or university to members of the public in a variety of forms, including degrees, certificate programs, credit and noncredit courses, workshops, seminars, online programs, and international initiatives.

Essential to all of these forms of education is substantive, valuable academic content. To bring such content to students and to develop innovative programs, CE units collaborate with academic departments at colleges and universities. Such partnerships provide excellent opportunities to extend the reach of higher education to new audiences, provide alternative educational delivery formats to students (such as online or hybrid classroom–online programs), and strengthen ties between CE units and academic departments.

The purpose of this chapter is to equip CE units and academic departments with information and ideas to help them more effectively develop and administer initiatives together. The chapter defines partnerships between academic departments and CE units, describes the kinds of programs that may be offered, discusses how such relationships are developed, explains the benefits that a CE unit can bring to partnerships with academic departments, details contractual and financial arrangements, examines issues that may arise, and summarizes suggested practices that can contribute to successful partnerships.

Definition

A partnership between a CE unit and an academic department is one in which both units work together to create, staff, approve, deliver, and administer programs to students. Such partnerships involve a range of individuals, including department chairs, professors, students, administrators, academic advisors, student affairs professionals, information technology specialists, and marketing and communications experts. Whether a partnership involves units within a college or university (the focus of this chapter) or internal units and external parties, the purpose of collaborating is the same: to succeed by harnessing the power of more than one set of minds and resources. The observation of Allen, Tilghman, and Whitaker (2010) in their article about collaboration between CE units and external organizations also applies to endeavors involving CE units and academic departments: Partnerships "can benefit all sides by helping them to achieve objectives that they could not have achieved themselves" (p. 109).

Kinds of Programs Offered

Programs developed by CE units and academic departments include self-sustaining (fee-based) credit degrees and credit certificate programs; noncredit certificate programs and courses; and other credit or noncredit programs that serve a range of audiences (such as summer youth programs, programs in which high school students earn college credit, and Osher Lifelong Learning Institutes that provide educational opportunities to adult community members). CE units and academic departments can also partner together and with external organizations to provide online education to people living in communities near and far; massive open online courses (MOOCs), for example, use the Internet to deliver educational content to thousands of individuals (Heller, 2013). A self-sustaining program operates on the revenue generated by student course fees. In a public college or university, a self-sustaining program does not receive state funds.

How Relationships Are Developed

Strong, respectful relationships are a key part of successful partnerships between CE units and academic departments working together on any type of educational offering. Either party can initiate such a partnership; the need for collaboration may arise for a variety of reasons. In some cases, an academic department identifies a need and reaches out to the CE unit. In other cases, leaders at CE units may realize that a gap in programming exists; to close the gap, CE unit staff and faculty members in an academic department can collaborate to develop a new program. In still other cases, a combination of fiscal and academic reasons may motivate the formation of a partnership. For example, in a public college or university setting, an academic department facing a significant cut to its state-assisted budget may decide to transfer a degree program (formerly state-operated) to a model that is completely self-sustaining. A CE unit with expertise in managing fee-based degrees may be a good choice of partner in such a situation. In this case, a CE–department partnership can allow the department to continue to provide strong academic content to students and to support the program (and possibly other departmental activities) with the fee-based revenue that is received. In another case, a CE unit might see a community need for noncredit programming and approach the head of an academic department in order to draw on the ideas and expertise of faculty teaching in the field.

In general, a successful partnership between a CE unit and an academic department results from a clearly defined and targeted program, clear communication, a defined agreement and procedures, and—most important—a continuing focus on benefiting students enrolled in the collaborative program that results. For example, the University of Washington Professional and Continuing Education unit successfully partners with a range of academic departments to provide fee-based (self-sustaining) degree programs to students. Programs offered in partnership include such subjects as digital media, social work, public administration, and creative writing and poetics. In these and in other fee-based degrees, the academic unit provides the academic leadership for and content of the program, schedules courses and faculty, and provides student services such as advising. Among other services, the University of Washington CE unit prepares registration forms, provides registration services, coordinates marketing activities for the program, issues regular financial statements, and helps to resolve issues.

How can CE units form successful partnerships with academic departments? First, through personal contacts and conversations: If senior leaders at a CE unit cultivate strong, respectful, and ongoing relationships with department chairs, faculty, and administrators, conversations can follow about collaborative opportunities to advance the educational mission of the college or university.

Second, CE unit staff can reach out to their colleagues in academic units and develop positive working relationships as they jointly administer programs. Such positive relationships help programs function smoothly, since CE and academic department staff can draw on their familiarity with each other and with the program to jointly resolve issues that arise. Robust, resilient relationships are vital to the success of a partnership, both in launching a shared initiative and in addressing difficulties that occur once it is under way; as Moroney and Boeck (2012) note, "When a partnership problem or challenge inevitably arises, it will be the relationship, not the legal agreement [between or among the partners] that determines whether or not the partnership succeeds" (p. 115).

Third, a CE unit can arrange periodic meetings with campus departmental administrators to keep them apprised of developments at the CE unit and seek departmental advice on and approval of policy matters. At the University of Washington, for example, the CE unit holds periodic fee-based administrator forums where CE staff and senior academic department administrators discuss a range of matters including changes to policies and procedures. These forums allow CE units and academic departments to strengthen relationships, freely discuss topics of shared concern, and work together on developing and adjusting practices that affect both partners.

Finally, a CE unit can establish program approval processes that require academic department sign-off for a program to occur. For example, at the University of Washington, all programs administered by the CE unit require annual approval from an academic unit in order to proceed. Campus departments review program course content and instructors each year as well as the results of student course evaluations, when available. This structural requirement for annual departmental approval means that the CE unit and academic department regularly communicate about programs, which provides opportunities to improve existing programs and to talk about ideas for new initiatives. In this type of approval arrangement, the CE unit is not separated from the academic life of the university but is instead closely linked to it.

Benefits that a CE Unit Brings to Partnerships with Academic Departments

A CE unit provides a range of benefits to an academic department, which allows the academic department to better concentrate on the academic content and delivery of a program. Examples of some benefits that a CE unit can provide are described next.

Market Research Expertise. CE units conduct market research studies to determine program viability. For instance, a CE research unit can administer a survey designed to determine if an audience exists for a program. CE research units can also gather and summarize secondary research relevant to a proposed program, such as employment outlook statistics, newspaper articles, numbers of related job postings online, and the content of related programs at other institutions. Once a program is under way, the CE unit market research team can administer a variety of surveys to help assess how the program is working, including surveys of program applicants, surveys of accepted students who chose other programs, and exit surveys of program graduates. The results of all of these surveys can assist academic units as they make decisions about program content, direction, and procedures.

Technology Expertise. CE units provide staff, software tools, and facilities to design, develop, and deliver academic content. The online learning team at a professional and CE unit can help online course developers and faculty design the structure of an online course, assemble its components (including text, illustrations, online discussion forums, and learning activities), post course materials online, and provide technical assistance to students and faculty once the course begins. CE units may also equip and staff specialized classrooms for delivery of hybrid instruction, which allow students physically present in a classroom and students online to simultaneously participate in a class session and, later, to review archived video and related course materials at their convenience. For example, the Harvard University Division of Continuing Education (DCE) collaborated with Harvard College faculty members to deliver undergraduate courses online to an audience that included Harvard University Extension School students; to do so, the DCE contributed staff expertise as well as funds for classroom and distance education production resources (Laserna & Leitner, 2008).

Marketing Expertise. A professional marketing team in a CE unit effectively spreads the word about programs to a wide audience. CE marketing staff can publish and mail annual and/or quarterly catalogs to the public, send e-mail messages and newsletters to prospective students, create and publish program Web sites and brochures, buy print advertisements, purchase ads on local mass transit systems and in regional broadcast media markets, and staff a call-in center to answer common questions about a range of programs. Individual programs and academic departments can benefit from the expertise, creative talent, customer relationship management systems, and established community presence of the CE marketing team, thereby freeing each academic unit from these tasks to concentrate on delivery of the program. For example, as McClure and Miller (2011) note in their article about a collaboration among the University of Massachusetts Amherst departments of Architecture + Design and Public History, the university's Continuing & Professional Education (CPE) unit, and Hancock Shaker Village to offer a master's degree program in historic preservation and architectural conservation, the marketing coordinator in the university's CPE unit "developed an in-depth marketing/advertising plan that addressed target populations, provided awareness and later details, contact information, and the value/importance of such a degree" (pp. 176–177).

Registration Expertise. CE units generate program registration forms and provide centralized services that allow students to enroll easily in a variety of types of programs using payment methods including cash, credit card, financial aid, and payment by third-party employers or organizations. CE units can also provide in-person and online registration options for programs as well as tools and reports that allow program staff to view and manage registration activities and enrollments easily.

Contract and Intellectual Property Expertise. CE units help academic units manage the contractual and intellectual property arrangements associated with a program. For example, CE units have standardized contracts for program developers and instructors. A CE unit can also employ a contracts manager who helps to clarify and resolve issues related to contracts and intellectual property.

Financial Expertise. CE units provide templates and guidelines for creating program budgets. Also, CE units prepare and assist with the analysis of financial statements for a program and transfer net revenue (gross revenue less expenses) to academic units. For example, the University of Washington

Professional and Continuing Education finance and planning team has developed standard computer-based budget spreadsheet templates. CE program management staff and academic departments use these templates to create, adjust, and review proposed program budgets before they are finalized. The standard template design allows CE staff to use a consistent, familiar model for budgeting and easily share information with academic departments. Also, the University of Washington CE finance and planning team provides monthly financial statements for each fee-based degree program, which allow campus academic units to see actual results to date compared to budgeted amounts.

Policy Expertise. CE units provide knowledge and facilitate connections with relevant university offices when questions about university policy arise. For example, I serve as the fee-based degree liaison at the University of Washington Professional and Continuing Education. In this role, I communicate with the university graduate school, financial aid office, registrar's office, and other units about a range of policy topics. Also, I help colleagues in the continuing education academic programs unit locate relevant policy information, and I am responsible for maintaining and editing materials about fee-based degree policies that are available to anyone on campus. If a CE unit staffs a policy liaison position in this manner, questions and issues can be resolved quickly.

Contractual Arrangements

Collaboration between an academic department and a CE unit benefits from clearly defined arrangements about program scope, instruction, and finances. In the case of noncredit programs, such arrangements may be relatively informal. In the case of credit certificate programs or credit fee-based degree programs, it is beneficial to specify arrangements in a formal memorandum of agreement (MOA; also called a memorandum of understanding), which is reviewed and signed by academic department, CE, and university leaders and generally is valid for a defined period of time (such as five years). A clearly defined MOA can pave the way for a successful partnership and promote thinking about (and resolution of) potential difficulties before a program begins.

Each MOA is unique, but it is useful for a CE unit to offer a standard MOA template that covers the essential elements of an agreement between the CE unit and the academic department. These are:

- Program name and description
- Faculty staffing and funding arrangements
- Student requirements for program completion
- Registration policies
- Services provided by each partner to the agreement
- Program administration fees charged by the CE unit

- Procedures for handling program financial surpluses and deficits
- Procedures for resolving issues not specifically discussed in the MOA

Two sections of an MOA deserve special attention. First, the MOA should describe how departmental faculty in a program will be supported if the program is discontinued. If the department, or its school or college, will assume responsibility for the salary and benefits of the program faculty, such arrangements should be noted. Second, the MOA should describe how to handle program deficits. If the program loses money, two scenarios can occur: planned and unplanned deficits. If a program has a planned deficit (e.g., because the program incurs expenses before the first group of students begins classes), the planned deficit can be carried forward and deducted from revenues in later years. If a program has an unplanned deficit (e.g., due to a significant, unexpected drop in enrollment), the MOA can state that the CE unit will absorb the deficit. Both types of financial assistance can be of great benefit to academic departments. In particular, in situations where a CE unit has set aside financial reserves to absorb unplanned deficits, the academic department can avoid a financial crisis and gain time to make adjustments that may help the program regain financial health. Regardless of the type of deficit that might occur, the CE unit and the academic department should monitor the fiscal health of the program carefully in order to minimize and quickly address any losses.

Financial Arrangements

Financial arrangements for collaborations between academic departments and CE units can vary. For example, at the end of a fiscal year, a noncredit program may not return any net revenue to an academic department; instead, all net revenue may remain with the CE unit. A fee-based degree program, however, might return any net revenue to the department at the end of a fiscal year. Clear descriptions of how financial arrangements are to be handled should be agreed on and included in a formal MOA for the program.

Additional aspects of financial arrangements between a CE unit and an academic department are described next.

Financial Reporting. A CE unit can provide monthly or quarterly financial statements, which help an academic department monitor the health of the program. Ideally, both a CE program manager and a fiscal analyst in the academic department will review the statement each month; two sets of eyes reviewing the data are more likely to identify errors.

Reducing Financial Risk. If a CE unit wishes to do so, it can set aside funds to help launch brand-new programs and provide financial assistance in case a program incurs a loss or needs to close. To set aside such funds, a CE unit can charge each fee-based program a percentage of gross revenue in each year that the program generates a positive return, with the percentage declining to zero over a period of time. For example, in Year 1 of a program,

6% of gross revenue can be charged; in Year 2, 5%; in Year 3, 4%; and so on. All such funds collected go into one pot and can be used to assist any program that meets need criteria defined by the CE unit.

Funding Faculty. Fee-based degree programs on which academic departments and CE units collaborate can be set up to help support faculty in academic departments. For example, a fee-based degree program can bear the entire cost of Faculty Member A (salary and benefits). In return, the academic department agrees to provide a specified number of courses, to be taught in the fee-based program by other departmental Faculty Members B, C, D, and E (who are not necessarily funded by the fee-based program). The academic department benefits because the entire cost of one faculty member (who may teach in a variety of programs) is financially supported by the fee-based program; the fee-based program benefits because it can draw on the expertise of a range of faculty members already at the college or university. At the University of Washington, for example, the fee-based undergraduate Evening Degree bachelor's completion program—a collaboration between the College of Arts and Sciences and the university's Professional and Continuing Education unit—funds several academic department faculty lines in this manner.

Overall, CE units and academic departments should communicate regularly about the financial status of a program in order to monitor its progress and make adjustments as needed. When a CE unit provides monthly financial statements that show budgeted amounts versus actual results, the task of monitoring the fiscal health of a program becomes easier than it would be without such statements, and problems can be spotted quickly.

Issues

However much academic departments and CE units may desire a problem-free partnership, no arrangement or MOA can foresee or prevent every issue that might arise. Issues between CE units and academic departments that may require resolution are discussed next.

Unsuitability for Partnership. Not all programs are a good fit for a partnership between an academic department and a CE unit. Sometimes staff in either unit may propose a partnership whose future success is questionable. For example, if an existing program can operate successfully under its current arrangements, it may be best to leave it as is. Also, CE units and academic departments should examine the motives for a partnership on a new or existing program carefully. Ultimately, the partnership should be embarked on if it will benefit students and support a sustainable program over the long term. By contrast, a partnership designed primarily with a fiscal motivation in mind (e.g., to help the academic department or CE unit increase short-term revenue or fill an immediate budget gap) should be examined carefully to determine whether it is reasonable to proceed.

Difficulty with Communication. Clear, frequent communication about partnerships is essential for success. If goals and objectives are unclear, if responsibilities are not clearly defined, and if financial arrangements are vague, difficulties can arise. Timelines, procedural checklists, formal MOAs, and other written communication can help avoid such difficulties. Also, confirming that all partners are of like mind about terminology can be beneficial; for example, in the University of Massachusetts Amherst collaboration described earlier, differing understandings of "student," "courses," and "credit hours" existed (McClure & Miller, 2011, p. 178). Most important, in-person meetings and telephone conversations can help prevent and resolve problems. Speaking together about an issue often can quickly clear up misunderstandings and help determine next steps. In addition, publishing standard policies related to programs offered in partnership can help to avoid and resolve communication difficulties. As noted, for example, the University of Washington Professional and Continuing Education unit publishes a "Fee-Based Degree Policy Notebook" on a Web site that is available to anyone on campus.

Dissatisfaction with Partnership. In some cases, faculty or staff in an academic department may view a partnership with a CE unit as undesirable. Academic department members may ask, for example, "Could we not offer this program solely through the department? Why is the CE unit charging us fees for administering this program? Could working with the CE unit diminish the prestige of the department?" Similarly, a CE unit may be dissatisfied with the direction or results of a partnership with an academic unit. A CE unit may ask, for example, "Why is the CE unit involved with a program that does not appear to serve a continuing education audience and is regularly losing money, with few signs of positive change from the academic department?" Ultimately, either partner retains the power to discontinue or dissolve their collaboration, if the partnership MOA so specifies. In any case, issues can be more quickly resolved if CE units and academic departments carefully listen to concerns that are raised, work to identify their root causes, seek to find common ground and positive solutions, and consider the value and benefits of the partnership as well as its drawbacks. A balanced, clear-headed, and considerate conversation about present dissatisfaction can help both partners alleviate concerns, promote goodwill, and make good decisions about next steps.

Conclusion: Building Successful Partnerships

Overall, this chapter has described a range of items and issues involved in developing and sustaining partnerships between academic departments and CE units. A successful partnership delivers an excellent educational experience to students, is fiscally sound over the long term, and draws on the strengths of the department and CE unit in order to make the most effective use of the talents and knowledge that reside in each group. For example, partners in the Harvard University collaboration described earlier combined the teaching strengths of Harvard College and the distance education resources of the university's Division of Continuing Education to extend educational opportunities to people around the globe (Laserna & Leitner, 2008).

The actions and attitudes that contribute to building successful partnerships are woven into the preceding discussion; to summarize, the most important are:

1. Work together to clearly define, target, and sustain programs that have as their primary goal the benefit of students.
2. Develop and maintain respectful, professional relationships through in-person meetings and attention to building a positive working collaboration.
3. Communicate clearly and in a timely manner.
4. Use a formal agreement (such as an MOA) and defined administrative and fiscal policies and procedures to effectively operate collaborative programs.
5. Facilitate collaboration and communication by requiring academic department approval for offerings administered through the CE unit.
6. If possible, create financial arrangements at the CE unit that reduce risk and assist academic departments when the need arises.
7. When problems occur, identify solutions together in an open, positive, and considerate spirit.

When academic departments and CE units work together in the manner just discussed, many benefits result:

- Students receive valuable knowledge and skills with which to reach their academic and personal goals.
- Faculty share their expertise and gain insights from their interactions with students.
- Departmental and CE unit staff enjoy the satisfaction of operating effective and successful programs.
- Colleges and universities broaden their reach to new audiences.
- Communities and societies benefit from the increased diffusion and application of knowledge.

References

Allen, N. H., Tilghman, C., & Whitaker, R. (2010). For gain or pain? Establishing effective partnerships with outside organizations. *Continuing Higher Education Review, 74*, 101–109. Retrieved from http://www.eric.ed.gov/ERICWebPortal/detail?accno=EJ907254

Heller, N. (2013, May 20). Laptop U: Has the future of college moved online? *The New Yorker, 89*(14), 80–91.

Laserna, C., & Leitner, H. (2008). Bit by bit: Innovating at the periphery to extend Harvard's core. *Continuing Higher Education Review, 72*, 163–183. Retrieved from http://www.eric.ed.gov/ERICWebPortal/detail?accno=EJ903446

McClure, W. S., & Miller, M. R. (2011). University of Massachusetts Amherst: An innovative partnership. *Continuing Higher Education Review, 75,* 173–180. Retrieved from http://www.eric.ed.gov/ERICWebPortal/detail?accno=EJ967818

Moroney, P., & Boeck, D. (2012). Thriving in partnership: Models for continuing education. *Continuing Higher Education Review, 76,* 112–121. Retrieved from http://www.eric.ed.gov/ERICWebPortal/detail?accno=EJ1000657

ANTHONY M. ENGLISH, *EdD, is a program management director in the academic programs unit at the University of Washington Professional and Continuing Education.*

4

In American universities, early distance education needed both continuing education and academic departments for establishing institutional cooperation, developing quality standards, adapting to change, and finding a funding model. Today, the Internet and the need for additional revenue are driving new distance education models.

From Access to Excess: Changing Roles and Relationships for Distance Education, Continuing Education, and Academic Departments in American Universities

Judy Copeland Ashcroft

Introduction

To educate more people for a knowledge economy, higher education is expanding proven vehicles for increasing access to education through the development of distance education (DE) programs. Additionally, organizations outside higher education are investing in these efforts. For example, an article in the University Professional and Continuing Education Association (UPCEA) newsletter (2013) reported that the Alfred P. Sloan Foundation provided grant support for the creation of the Inter Organizational Task Force on Online Learning. UPCEA tapped Ray Schroeder, associate vice chancellor at the University of Illinois at Springfield, to serve as chair and convene the task force comprised of representatives from leading national organizations monitoring online and e-learning. Because many assume that DE is a recent option, Schroeder (UPCEA, 2013) reminded the task force of the importance of drawing on the "knowledge and experience of those who represent the colleges and universities who have demonstrated their commitment to quality and innovation in this field" (p. 1). For more than a century, American higher education has responded to the need for nontraditional education by offering both synchronous and asynchronous DE to overcome the barriers of time, place, pace, delivery, capacity, and cost.

Subsequently, the field of DE has created an international body of knowledge from both experience and research that informs today's best practices. Currently, American DE programs are also doing breakthrough work developing the capacity to provide convenient access to education for students of all ages, with differing learning styles and varying abilities to access technology. The dynamic DE programs at American universities are innovating to meet unique educational demands. Today's DE offers a solid foundation for nontraditional learning.

Three Forces

To appreciate this foundation, three different forces should be discussed: the growth of DE as an educational concept; the growth of continuing education (CE) programs within universities; and the growth of academic departments seeking to develop, administer, and market their own DE classes. Before DE was institutionalized, it was a vision, a social concept, and a powerful perceived solution to a need. Attempting to understand DE today can be a puzzling study because new iterations create a new vocabulary. For purposes of this discussion, *DE* means that the student and teacher are not in the same place at the same time for instruction; consequently, teaching by correspondence, teaching with media, and teaching online are all forms of DE. More specific definitions of terms associated with DE can be found in a comprehensive Glossary of Terms developed by Michael Simonson (2008) located on the United States Distance Learning Association site.

After the Morrill Act in 1862, CE within universities became a counterpoint to the academic departments because it could respond quickly to opportunities, partner with all parts of the university, and work as an entrepreneurial unit. Comprehending CE today can be challenging because it has many names including extension, lifelong learning, and adult education. In the *Handbook of Adult and Continuing Education*, Thomas M. Hatfield (1989) addressed the diversity of terms used by explaining that they "usually reflect only minor differences in concept or in philosophy because an aim of virtually all adult and continuing education programs is to provide an organized learning experience for individuals who are beyond usual college age and who are not regularly enrolled students in a college or university" (p. 303). Thus, *CE* is also a broad term.

The third force is the academic department, one of the most established and autonomous parts of a university. During the 20th century, when DE was developing in American universities, an academic department was usually similar to the definition in the Academic Charter of Bowling Green State University (Bowling Green State University, 1991). Article XI states that an academic department is "the basic administrative unit within the University organized to carry on and develop the instructional and research activities of its faculty" (para. 1). For the development of DE, the academic department's responsibility for instructional activities—teaching, evaluating, and awarding degrees—proves to be critical.

Institutional Cooperation

Just as the economy now needs more Americans with in-demand skills, the industrial economy of the 19th century also required changes in curricula and in capacity. What lessons can be learned from the way American universities responded to this earlier need? The aim of DE was to provide persons geographically separated from classroom instruction with access to current information. For the agricultural economy, colleges and universities shared their academic resources through academic professors who traveled to communities to lecture. After rural mail delivery was established, faculty added instructing students through correspondence, which "provided educational independence for the learner" (Garrison, 1989, p. 223). Higher education knew a demonstrated need existed, but there was little institutional infrastructure to administer or fund this new DE concept. Within institutions, CE programs were the group usually charged with providing the service prong of the mission, and they were already providing access to nontraditional education by teaching adult students in the community. Consequently, CE expanded into offering noncredit DE courses for professional or personal development. However, a critical juncture was reached when distance learners wanted to take courses for college credit. Awarding credit is the responsibility of and is controlled by academic departments, and these departments, chairs, and faculty were concerned about becoming involved in such a nontraditional program. Taylor (2010) describes how universities and academic departments were influenced by the philosophy of Immanuel Kant, who envisioned a university that educated the masses; therefore, efficiency would come from division of labor "into separate departments and subdepartments, each of which has different expertise, tasks and responsibilities" (p. 52). Thus, academic departments, based on centuries of mass production, and continuing education, based on meeting nontraditional students' current needs, often found each other's positions incomprehensible; however, they were in unknown territory where the assessment standards from institutions and accrediting bodies did not yet include DE. Also, for academic departments to offer DE, they would need an entrepreneurial, administrative infrastructure. CE did have an infrastructure, but it could not offer DE credit courses without faculty from the academic departments. Eventually, a key partnership for DE evolved: academic departments provide advising, curriculum, instruction, evaluation, and credit while CE provides support through student services, faculty support, and business management. The first lesson learned was that each partner needed to make changes and cooperate in step-by-step problem solving to offer DE.

Quality Standards

Many students benefited from these DE courses, but the partnership remained an uneasy one. DE kept growing and changing, and the differences between a traditional academic department and a nontraditional CE group kept a constant tension in the partnership until standards of quality were established. The element of "distance" introduced significant challenges; thus, DE was defining itself through both comparison to the classroom and contrast with what distance students needed. Members of the faculty were concerned about the academic quality of the new program; they wanted to know how faculty were chosen, what qualifications were required, how faculty were evaluated, how the work of distance students compared to the work of traditional students, how the program assured that the student receiving the grade was the student doing the work, what research on DE showed, and what the retention and completion rates were.

Peer Review. CE professionals, who were DE experts and also members of the Independent Study Division of UPCEA, began an additional layer of quality control: peer review. Representing large DE programs at leading institutions, including Brigham Young University, Penn State University, Texas Tech University, the University of California–Berkeley, the University of Florida, the University of Missouri–Columbia, the University of Nebraska–Lincoln, and the University of Texas at Austin, the experts met multiple times a year to discuss, debate, and refine best practices for self-paced DE. In this process, the quality questions that faculty asked were also examined. Consequently, consensus was found on some points. For example, qualified instructors who were not faculty could teach noncredit courses; however, credit courses would come from the institution's faculty in an organized academic department. An excellent student learning experience required a well-designed course and study guide, timely faculty feedback, and the support of a knowledgeable student services staff. To verify a student's identity, a photo ID was required for presentation prior to the in-person proctored final examination; and a student must earn a passing grade on the final examination to receive credit for the course. These concepts helped shape the foundation for much of DE today. Documents from this period of DE growth are in the National University Extension Association Records, Special Collections Research Center, Syracuse University Library. Processed holdings are at http://library.syr.edu/digital/guides/n/nuea.htm.

Research. Academic research also helps distinguish quality education. The *Continuing Higher Education Review* (*CHER*) is in its 77th year of publication. As the professional journal of the UPCEA, CHER is instrumental in sharing research and ideas and helps shape the discipline of DE. As a result of research on the use of technology in teaching, DE professionals agreed that technology is not used for the sake of using technology; in other words, a DE course is not an online course but rather it is a well-designed course offered online. The quality standard is that technology serves teaching; thus, faculty and instructional designers decide which technologies best enhance teaching content and achieving learning outcomes. Studies on DE were plentiful, but research dramatically increased following the 1999 release of *The No Significant Difference Phenomenon*, edited by Thomas L. Russell. Today, scholars consult the Western Interstate Commission for Higher Education (WICHE) Cooperative for Educational Technologies (WCET), which maintains a robust Web site for No Significant Difference and related research at http://nosignificantdifference.org/.

These quality concepts began as someone's idea for teaching students at a distance while upholding academic integrity. The ideas that worked evolved into national best practices and provided a foundation that not only helped students learn but also respected the role of faculty. A second lesson learned was that higher education institutions require assurance of quality, and in a new field, the partners must help establish the standards.

Continuous Change

Significant strides in instructional practice, peer review, and research were helping create and document quality in DE just as more changes came. The introduction of technology on campuses quickly created added possibilities and concerns. Continuing educators are early adopters and eager experimenters in their quest for improving courses. However, faculty feared that new technologies were dictating how to teach, and teaching was their departmental expertise. This evolutionary step in DE's measured growth was a small tremor compared to the quake of digital technology that became pervasive not only in DE delivery but also in the university environment. In truth, technology was beginning its disruption in education. Christensen, Horn, and Johnson (2011) describe disruptive innovation as taking something that was historically expensive, complicated, and available to only a few and making it affordable and accessible. The Internet, the first of two significant game changers for DE in higher education, continues to influence teaching and learning. Online technology became central to university administration, marketing, and admissions in the 1990s and resulted in institutions hiring chief information technology officers (CIOs), who supported new technology, technology-enhanced classrooms, and learning management systems (LMS). The LMS was originally provided for campus use; however, when faculty and instructional designers recognized the potential, the LMS became the dominant delivery platform for DE because it offered instruction closer to the face-to-face experience. The third lesson learned was that the provision of DE requires the ability to adapt to consistent, continuous change.

Profit

In the partnership with academic departments, the entrepreneurial CE unit usually managed the business, most often on a cost recovery or self-funded model. However, with the trend of reduced state funding for higher education, the need for new revenue gained importance. Additionally, businesses ventured into the education sector with online universities as direct competitors. The for-profit universities found a need that higher education was not serving adequately: the working adult. For a while, for-profits, state universities, and private institutions lived in parallel, but that ended when the U.S. economy went into recession.

A second game changer for DE was the weak U.S. economy following the recession in 2007. A college president, James Garland (2009), analyzed the plight of universities in *Saving Alma Mater: A Rescue Plan for America's Public Universities* and concluded that states, federal government, and taxpayers cannot increase funding to higher education because "powerful demographic, social, and economic forces that had nothing to do with higher education" have left all sources short of funds (p. xi). The slow recovery, specifically the high unemployment rates, plus a divisive and extended political campaign brought additional challenges to higher education.

Administrators observed the for-profits and saw a new role for university DE: creating recurring revenue streams for the institution. Like the introduction of technology, this need for additional funds spawned a second surge of interest in online programs: DE programs delivered on the Internet. Most CE distance education programs share residual revenue with the institution and the academic departments, but the difference between sharing residual and being required to earn recurring revenue to help offset budget shortfalls is very distinct. As DE programs worked vigorously to increase enrollments without having additional funds for market research, targeted multimedia recruitment campaigns, and a skilled sales staff, the disparities between university programs and for-profits became clear. The cost recovery business model was not a business plan for generating significant profit. The complexities of funding increased with the open education resource movement. Intellectual property is a treasure of higher education, but when MIT posted courses on the Web, free to anyone who wished to see them, the paradigm changed. According to Peter Smith (2010), "making this material available will indirectly drive a new and enhanced focus on new forms of learning and organizing education. These forms will include the assessment of learning, personalized services, and academic planning as separate but essential parts of the educational experience" (p. 124).

Hoping DE could generate profits elsewhere, some institutions reorganized, breaking the partnership between CE and academic departments and moving their DE from CE to the CIO portfolios, to centers for teaching effectiveness, or to new stand-alone DE units. Some courses were returned to the academic departments. The need for excess revenue (profit) changed the role of university DE from primarily providing access for nontraditional students to marketing online courses that generate recurring revenue, even as more costly barriers were imposed. For example, the U.S. Department of Education (2010) issued Program Integrity Rules intended to control the for-profits, but the unintended consequence quickly placed all postsecondary institutions in an untenable and costly position of petitioning each state for authorization to deliver DE. For-profits were some of the first to comply with the new regulations. The fourth lesson learned was that finding a sustainable business model for DE is one of the most vexing challenges.

Transitions

Continuing education has a history of rapidly changing to satisfy student and university needs while also staying financially viable. Currently, the larger academic environment is finding it necessary to make changes in response to the disruption of the Internet and the pressures of a struggling economy.

Institutional Acceptance. Some positive signs suggest that DE is in a period of transition, moving from the margin to the mainstream. University administration welcomed the implementation by the National Center for Education Statistics of a new DE definition for the 2011–2012 Integrated Post-secondary Data Education System (IPEDS); the definition begins: "Education that uses one or more technologies to deliver instruction to students who are separated from the instructor and to support regular and substantive interaction between the students and the instructor synchronously or asynchronously" (National Center for Education Statistics, 2012, "Distance education"). This change recognizes not only the impact of technology but also the importance of the services CE has been providing, especially the "substantive interaction" through instructional design, faculty interaction, and student support communication. With IPEDS, DE statistics look more like information on traditional courses.

Anticipation. Fortunately, new DE offerings are getting a quick start by building on lessons learned from previous DE programs. Not only are academics more accepting of online courses for students, but many are creating and teaching their own online courses using programs similar to those developed by Quality Matters (n.d.), an international organization that supports peer review of online courses and also certifies the design of online courses. New ideas have additional advantages, including willing faculty uniquely prepared to lead because they are currently teaching in technology-enriched classrooms, communicating with students online and on social media, and using outcomes-based assessment of student learning. New programs should have fewer quality questions to answer because highly respected universities, including MIT, Stanford, Harvard, Berkeley, Princeton, the University of Washington, the University of Wisconsin–Extension, and Georgia Tech, are launching innovative DE and e-learning programs. Subscribing to the Professional, Continuing, and Online Education Update by UPCEA at continuingedupdate.blogspot.com is an efficient way to keep abreast through daily updates of news, research, and trends. Importantly, a global student population, skilled in using the Internet and online technologies, is anticipating enrolling in these offerings.

Flexibility. Just as higher education is making changes and incorporating DE, so is the U.S. Department of Education. The Southern New Hampshire (SNHU) Communications Office (2013) reported that the Department of Education was looking favorably at a proposal from SNHU "to award aid based on the direct assessment of student learning" (para. 7). Endorsing competency-based education is a fundamental change from the credit hour measure that is currently used. Furthermore, the possibility of students in competency-based programs receiving federal student aid is an even greater change. The Department of Education is changing a paradigm to make today's DE even more relevant, especially for adult students.

Finding Balance. Not only is DE in a time of rapid change and transition, but the educational environment is changing too. It is necessary to find a balance that meets the needs of state legislators, business leaders, and public education. Government and business are championing a curriculum with six attributes:

1. Fully online courses
2. Proctored online examinations with student verification
3. Competency-based outcomes
4. Accelerated courses of no more than five weeks
5. Concierge student service
6. Degrees aligned with workforce demands

The business community, including technology and manufacturing sectors, needs more people with specialized skills and is lobbying for changes, including helping adults who previously earned college credits quickly complete degrees needed in the professional workforce. Higher education is responding; the Florida Senate (2013) Web site describes the Florida Degree Completion Pilot Project that addresses these needs.

The role of faculty and their relationship to a department is being redefined. Sebastian Thrun, director of the Stanford Artificial Intelligence Laboratory, experimented with a free massive open online course (MOOC) on artificial intelligence, and more than 160,000 students in more than 190 countries enrolled (Udacity, n.d.). Following the success of the MOOC, Thrun formed Udacity, a company that offers noncredit MOOCs free to students, with the mission "to bring accessible, affordable, engaging and effective higher education to the world" (Udacity, n.d., para. 1). This MOOC experiment addressed the distance education issues of access, relevance, and efficiency/cost. Anyone, anywhere who could log on could participate. The content was rigorous, relevant, and in demand and taught by a skilled expert. Technologies yielded efficiency, and the cost to students was affordable—only their time and intellectual engagement; enrolling was free. Because no departmental course and curriculum committee approved or awarded credit, students who passed the course received not Stanford credit but a certificate of completion. Around the world, students voted with their keypads: The reputation of the instructor was more compelling than credit from a regionally accredited institution. However, on January 15, 2013, it was announced that through a partnership with San Jose State University, Udacity students could convert passing to college credit for $150 (San Jose State University, 2013). Thrun (2013) also discussed a collaboration with Georgia Tech and AT&T on a new online master's degree program. Faculty members are now literally outside the box, including Kant's compartmentalized departments.

Determining the acceptable percentage of outsourced work and monitoring the effectiveness of corporate partnerships is another emerging challenge requiring balance. The role of corporate partners may increase as universities strive to meet the Lumina Foundation's (n.d.) Goal 2025: "to increase the proportion of Americans with high-quality college degrees, certificates and credentials to 60 percent by 2025." Allen, Tilghman, and Whitaker (2010) point out that CE and DE programs have experience with vendors and consultants but warn that "partnerships run deeper and include formulation of strategy, interdependence, and higher levels of trust between organizations" (p. 109). Universities must be protective of their students' personal information, but the boundary will be tested as corporate software programs can now organize big data sets to produce predictive analytics on a granular level for administrative decision making.

Alone or in partnership with others, CE's role continues to be providing access to relevant education. In fact, most of what business is asking for is offered currently through CE, the part of the university that can be entrepreneurial in meeting individual and community needs. With its diverse portfolio and ability to offer noncredit courses on flexible calendars on site or online, CE's role is expanding. At the same time, CE may see its DE mission adopted by others. Like Udacity in its mission statement, Coursera, a social entrepreneur offering MOOCs, describes itself on its Web site with vocabulary that is very much the language of continuing educators, including "everyone has access" to education (Coursera, n.d., para. 3).

Conclusion

Despite challenges, higher education continues to provide quality instruction because adults as well as students of traditional age want and need to learn. The original role of DE—to provide access to quality education—is still valid because globally connected economies need universal access to create and sustain a large, highly skilled workforce. Individuals need the most recent and relevant information explained by the best thinkers and teachers, instantly available at all times on personal devices wherever students are and preferably at no cost. The Do It Yourself University that education futurist Anya Kamenetz envisioned in her 2010 book, *DIY U: Edupunks, Edupreneurs and the Coming Transformation of Higher Education*, is manifesting now. Current changes are driven by the challenge to improve the national economy by preparing highly skilled employees for American business and accelerating the graduation of students who will be in demand for their skills. Changing needs are a social and economic constant, so as new requirements are presented to higher education, the DE model offers lessons for success.

References

Allen, H. A., Tilghman, C., & Whitaker, R. (2010). For gain or pain? Establishing effective partnerships with outside organizations. *Continuing Higher Education Review, 74*(Fall), 101–109.

Bowling Green State University. (1991). Article XI: The academic departments. *Academic charter*. Retrieved from www.bgsu.edu/downloads/bgsu/file896.pdf

Christensen, C. M., Horn, M. B., & Johnson, C. W. (2011). *Disrupting class: How disruptive innovation will change the way the world learns*. New York, NY: McGraw-Hill.

Coursera. (n.d). *About us*. Retrieved from https://www.coursera.org/about

Florida Senate. (2013). *Florida Degree Completion Pilot Program*. Retrieved from http://www.flsenate.gov/laws/statutes/2012/1006.735

Garland, J. C. (2009). *Saving alma mater: A rescue plan for America's public universities*. Chicago, IL: University of Chicago Press.

Garrison, D. R. (1989). Distance education. In S. B. Merriam & P. M. Cunningham (Eds.), *Handbook of adult and continuing education* (pp. 221–232). San Francisco, CA: Jossey-Bass.

Hatfield, T. M. (1989). Four-year colleges and universities. In S. B. Merriam & P. M. Cunningham (Eds.), *Handbook of adult and continuing education* (pp. 303–315). San Francisco, CA: Jossey-Bass.

Kamenetz, A. (2010). *DIY U: Edupunks, edupreneurs, and the coming transformation of higher education*. White River Junction, VT: Chelsea Green.

Lumina Foundation. (n.d.). Retrieved from http://www.luminafoundation.org/goal_2025.html

National Center for Education Statistics. (2012). *Integrated postsecondary education data system glossary*. Washington, DC: U.S. Department of Education. Retrieved from http://nces.ed.gov/ipeds/glossary/?charindex=D

Quality Matters. (n.d.). *About us*. Retrieved from https://www.qualitymatters.org/About

Russell, T. L. (Ed.). (1999). *The no significant difference phenomenon*. Raleigh, NC: North Carolina University.

San Jose State University (SJSU). (2013, January 15). *San Jose State University and Udacity announce partnership to pilot for-credit online courses to expand access to higher education*. Retrieved from http://blogs.sjsu.edu/today/2013/sjsu-and-udacity-partnership/

Simonson, M. (2008). *Distance learning glossary*. Retrieved from http://www.usdla.org/assets/pdf_files/Glossary_Distance.pdf

Smith, P. (2010). *Harnessing America's wasted talent: A new ecology of learning*. San Francisco, CA: Jossey-Bass.

SNHU Communications Office. (2013, March 19). *"Chronicle" and "Inside Higher Ed" laud SNHU's model of competency-based education*. Retrieved from http://www.snhu.edu/16308.asp

Taylor, M. C. (2010). *Crisis on campus: A bold plan for reforming our colleges and universities*. New York, NY: Knopf.

Thrun, S. (2013, June 24). Sebastian Thrun: Thoughts and financial transparency on our masters in computer science with Georgia Tech. *Udacity*. Retrieved from http://blog.udacity.com/2013/06/sebastian-thrun-thoughts-and-financial.html#sthash.sDWj0gMn.dpuf

Udacity. (n.d.). *About Udacity*. Retrieved from https://www.udacity.com/us#sec3

University Professional and Continuing Education Association (UPCEA). (2013, October 3). *Online learning organizations create a national e-learning alliance to promote access to quality*

higher education online. Retrieved from http://www.upcea.edu/content.asp?admin
=Y&pl=181& sl=176&contentid=284

U.S. Department of Education. (2010, October 28). *Department of Education establishes new student aid rules to protect borrowers and taxpayers*. Washington, DC. Retrieved from http://www.ed.gov/news/press-releases/department-education-establishes-new-student-aid-rules-protect-borrowers-and-tax

JUDY COPELAND ASHCROFT, *EdD, served as dean of continuing and innovative education at the University of Texas at Austin and as 2010–2011 president of the University Professional and Continuing Education Association.*

Central to many of the current developments in higher education is prior learning assessment (PLA). In the past several years, with new and ambitious degree completion goals for adults, the United States is witnessing what can only be called a surge of interest in PLA.

Growing Importance of Prior Learning Assessment in the Degree-Completion Toolkit

Rebecca Klein-Collins, Judith B. Wertheim

Starting in 1974, the Council for Adult and Experiential Learning (CAEL) has helped colleges and universities develop and expand their prior learning assessment (PLA) programs for adult and other nontraditional learners. PLA is the process by which an individual's learning is assessed and evaluated for purposes of granting college credit, certification, or advanced standing toward further education or training. That learning may have been acquired through on-the-job experiences, corporate training, military training or experience, volunteer work, or self-guided study. PLA methods include exams, individual portfolios, or the formal review of a course or training program to determine whether it is at the college level. Typically, the first two methods assess the learning outcomes or what the individual knows and can do; the last method assesses inputs, what materials, and learning activities a course or training program presents.

Recently, CAEL has seen a dramatic growth in interest in PLA—not just from colleges and universities but also from federal and state governments. PLA has been gaining respect and acceptance in higher education and the public sector, largely coinciding with the emphasis on improving rates of degree completion.

Given its long history of advocating for and supporting PLA programs in higher education, CAEL could not be more pleased to see the embrace of PLA and, with it, the growing understanding that what matters most is *what* someone has learned, not how or where they learned it. But CAEL is also mindful of other changes in higher education today, particularly those that are opening up educational resources and learning opportunities in ways that PLA practitioners could not have imagined a decade ago. These changes clearly indicate that there may be much more in store for PLA assessment methods and for adult learners who use this option in their degree plans. There is, in fact, a new, expanded future for PLA.

Background

In the past few years, many leaders in education, the public sector, and philanthropy have focused on the goal of better postsecondary degree completion. Indeed, even President Obama has addressed this as an important national goal. As noted by the National Commission on Higher Education Attainment in its January 23, 2013, open letter to college and university leaders, PLA has emerged as an important strategy for helping more people cross the finish line to degree completion. With PLA, someone with college-level learning acquired outside the classroom—on the job, in corporate training, in the military, through self-guided study—can earn credit for that learning through a variety of assessments. This is particularly true for adults who often return to school to complete a degree or credential, begin a degree, or change careers with substantial learning experiences that can be applied to their educational goals.

With credit earned through PLA, a student saves time and money in earning a degree. And perhaps buoyed by the recognition of having already mastered learning at the college level, that student is then motivated to persist and complete the degree. CAEL research on more than 62,000 adult students from 48 postsecondary institutions provides support for this supposition by showing that adult students with credit earned through PLA were two and a half times more likely to complete a degree compared to adult students without such credit (Klein-Collins, 2010). This was true for students regardless of race/ethnicity, age, financial aid status, or gender.

Several observations point to the current surge of interest in PLA:

- At CAEL's annual conference, there are increasing numbers of proposals for the PLA track, more attendees at PLA sessions and workshops, and a twofold increase in the attendance at a two-day preconference PLA workshop.
- Amendments to federal regulations encourage the use of PLA in workforce training programs. For example, in 2010, the U.S. Department of Labor's Training and Employment Guidance Letter 15-10 listed PLA as a strategy "to help adults and dislocated workers obtain academic credit for independently attained knowledge and skills, thereby accelerating the process of credential attainment" (p. 11). In addition, the department's recent Trade Adjustment Assistance Community College and Career Training Grant Programs listed "credit for prior learning" as a possible implementation measure (e.g., U.S. Department of Labor, 2013, p. 8).

- As they explore ways to promote greater access to PLA offerings throughout state institutions, state leaders also cite PLA. In July 2012, CAEL cohosted a meeting at Lumina Foundation for state leaders interested in learning more about PLA and how their states can promote its use at public postsecondary institutions (see Sherman, Klein-Collins, & Palmer, 2012, on existing state policy efforts as well as model state policies).
- In addition, media are devoting increased attention to PLA in reports about higher education; and CAEL has successfully launched Learning Counts.org, a national online portfolio development service.

It is tempting to conclude that PLA's time has come. However, it is worth considering whether we may be merely scratching the surface of what can be possible with PLA's tools for assessing student learning.

Vision of Expanded Uses for PLA

Right now, dramatic transformations are occurring in how postsecondary institutions deliver education, how they award credentials, and how they structure degree programs. There is greater access to open educational resources, from free learning materials to free online courses taught by professors from elite institutions. There is also greater understanding of the connections between learning and the workplace. Many of these developments involve new uses and applications for PLA assessment methods.

DIY Learning Option: OER and MOOCs. Before the technology revolution, the presumed users of PLA options were people who had acquired learning on the job, through volunteer work, through the military, or through self-guided study. Self-guided study was once only for the truly motivated, the self-starter of learning. Today, however, the lifelong learner has options for acquiring knowledge and new competencies in ways previously unimagined. Students of all ages now have access to open and free educational resources (OER), whether through YouTube videos, iTunes lectures, or the recent phenomenon of massive open online courses (MOOCs). Some of this learning is at the college level, and some is equivalent in its depth and breadth to existing college course offerings.

YouTube lectures, iTunesU, open textbooks, and other relatively new OER offerings make self-guided study a more accessible option for such do-it-yourselfers. Not only are these options readily available, online, and mostly free, but they provide guidance to the learner. Although they still require the student to be motivated and entrepreneurial in the approach to learning, the new options take some of the guesswork out of how to go about the learning process. And as has long been the case, PLA can then offer a way to have that learning formally recognized and applied to a degree.

The current standout among open education options is the MOOC. As millions of people throughout the world sign up for these courses, many of which are led by professors from elite institutions, a frequently heard question is, "How can someone earn college credit for what is learned in a MOOC?" In answer to this question, some individual postsecondary institutions are evaluating particular MOOC offerings in order to award credit to successful completers. In addition, organizations like CAEL and the American Council on Education are developing ways to assess the learning from MOOCs for the purposes of awarding college credit or validating well-defined competencies (Lederman, 2013). In this way, do-it-yourself, or DIY, education can be as much about working toward credentials as it is about learning.

Competency-Based Degree Programs. The emphasis on degree completion is partly about providing good career opportunities for Americans, but it is also about making sure our workforce is prepared to support the needs of the global economy. Ironically, the message about needing more college graduates comes at a time when both students and employers are beginning to question the value of a degree. Students wonder what they are getting in return for the high cost of tuition and student loan debt, and employers wonder whether someone with a postsecondary degree or credential is actually ready for the workplace. Both within and outside higher education, critics are asking, "What does a college graduate know? What can a college graduate do?"

In response to these concerns, educational thought leaders and individual postsecondary institutions are acknowledging that the old model of relying on the credit hour as a measure of student learning is no longer sufficient. Developed in the early 20th century, the credit hour was, in fact, never designed to be a measure of student learning. It is certainly not one today (Laitinen, 2012). In the 21st century, Lumina Foundation (2011), among other proponents of competencies, has proposed a new competency-based framework, the Degree Qualifications Profile, to promote a greater emphasis on defining and measuring what students learn at various levels of postsecondary education. Pioneering institutions are migrating away from the model that focuses on the accumulation of credit hours and toward something different: degrees based on demonstration of a predefined set of competencies. (To learn more about various models of these programs, see Klein-Collins, 2012.)

Competency-based programs share a philosophy with PLA: that what individuals know is more important than where or how they acquired that knowledge. In addition, competency-based programs are a natural fit with many methods of PLA because they assess the outcomes of student learning in a rigorous way. An important model of a competency-based degree program is one in which a student progresses not by satisfying a set of course requirements but by passing a series of competency-based assessments. With faculty guidance, the student acquires those competencies through traditional coursework, self-guided study, or workplace training or other life experience. The competency assessments essentially have the same function as PLA.

Until now, CAEL's PLA portfolio assessment process, through its LearningCounts.org PLA service, as well as through PLA training that CAEL offers to institutions, has taken a "course match" approach, in which a student's demonstrated learning is compared to the expected learning outcomes of existing courses at regionally accredited institutions. If a student can align learning with the learning outcomes of a particular course, and support it with documentation, the assessor can recommend a credit award for that course.

With the emergence of new competency-based degree programs across the country, CAEL sees the need for a portfolio assessment process that results in a transcript of both recommended course credits *and* demonstrated competencies. In some cases, this may require going beyond a student's written narrative and supporting documents to include video demonstrations, work products, and simulations. Students currently can take advantage of new technologies to provide supporting evidence of what they know, and CAEL plans to test additional new forms of performance assessment and assessor interviews.

As demonstrations of learning gain currency, CAEL recognizes that the word *prior* in "prior learning assessment" may no longer be relevant. The learning that is assessed could have been acquired years ago or minutes ago. Yet regardless of when the learning occurred, evaluating competencies can offer significant help in addressing the quality concerns about college degrees raised by employers and education consumers.

Student Mobility and Credit Transfer. In order to support degree completion, many state leaders have recognized the reality of, and challenges posed by, increased student mobility. The National Student Clearinghouse Research Center recently reported that one-third of all students changed institutions at some time before earning a degree (Hossler et al., 2012).

Today more students than ever before have acquired learning at more than one postsecondary institution, and these students often face institutional resistance when trying to apply all of their credits from various institutions toward their degrees. The solutions can involve articulation agreements between and among schools. These agreements spell out the courses that will transfer. However, when there is not a perfect match—when a course at College A does not perfectly match a course at College B—there can be problems. And although the course credits may be accepted, they may not necessarily apply to the degree, often requiring the student to study the same material again. In such cases, PLA can provide an alternate route. Imagine, for example, a student who has mastered four of the five required learning outcomes for a course. That student can independently learn the remaining required competencies and use PLA to demonstrate the new learning. By using the PLA option, students will not need to retake entire courses to have their previous learning fully recognized by the transfer institution.

Badges or Microcredentials. The online development organization Mozilla has joined forces with HASTAC (Humanities, Arts, Science, and Technology Advanced Collaboratory) and the John D. and Catherine T. MacArthur

Foundation to explore the concept of "badges," or microcredentials. This initiative is based on the idea that traditional measures of achievement—associate and bachelor's degrees, for example—may be too large a credentialing unit for some needs. Given the rapidly changing workplace, a microcredentialing system would provide greater flexibility for employers to specify exactly what skills and competencies are needed and would allow individuals the ability to customize their education and training to meet those specific needs (The Mozilla Foundation and Peer 2 Peer University, 2012).

Should a system for microcredentials develop, perhaps in conjunction with a strong move toward competencies within postsecondary education more generally, the metadata specifications associated with a badge (see https://wiki.mozilla.org/Badges/Onboarding-Issuer#E._Metadata_Spec) would specify the competencies needed, and PLA could provide ways for learners to demonstrate their skills and competencies to earn those badges, no matter where the learners acquired those skills and competencies.

Workforce Development. Similarly, the public workforce system could incorporate PLA methods into its short- and long-term training initiatives in order to determine what the participants already know and can do. PLA could help identify both acquired learning and whatever additional training participants still need. Such an approach would require a transformation of many current training programs so that they are more modular and competency based.

For job seekers with some previous experience or training, these changes in the workforce system could mean a shortened time to employability. For the public sector, this could mean a more efficient use of limited training resources. These benefits may underlie the rationale for the 2010 U.S. Department of Labor's Training and Employment Guidance Letter 15–10, referenced earlier in this chapter. Some states, such as Indiana, already encourage consideration of PLA when awarding a job seeker any public workforce training dollars through an Individual Training Account.

Worker-to-Workplace Connection. The prior learning portfolio has shown additional utility for job seekers and incumbent workers. For example, the workforce system might consider the assessment of an individual's learning portfolio as the foundation for helping to connect job seekers to employers in new ways. The learning portfolio, once developed, could be expanded to include future training interests, previous work-related accomplishments, and otherwise "packaging" the job seeker for the labor market. In other words, the portfolio could be a new kind of résumé that conveys more concrete information about a job seeker's competencies, skills, previous experience, and potential for growth.

Portfolios, specifically e-portfolios, currently are used by many college students not only to demonstrate learning outcomes of the complement of their degree studies but also to market themselves to prospective employers. The portfolios package learning that takes place in all environments, with evidence such as student achievements, highlights of coursework, videos of music performances, presentation slides, and other digital content produced by the student independently or as part of formal education. Portfolios are then used by the graduating students in their job search. The workforce system could encourage its job-seeking clients to showcase their skills, competencies, and achievements to prospective employers in an e-portfolio, either alongside a more traditional résumé or as a substitute for one. The portfolio has the potential to provide valuable additional information to prospective employers, not just on job-specific skills and competencies but also the softer skills that employers care so much about, such as critical thinking, problem solving, communication, working in teams, and skills, along with knowledge of a specific discipline.

Once the individual is employed, the portfolio can be used as a human resources management tool. It can be designed to capture not only existing skills, competencies, and accomplishments but also to present the employee's pathway to career and educational goals. It can track learning and skill needs, with connections to career pathways within a company or an industry. These portfolios could then be synced to the company's learning management system for better delivery and management of company talent development, even connecting workers with new assignments that help them acquire new skills not typically associated with their current position. This process opens up possibilities for lateral movement within the company as well as more traditional career pathways.

While some of this repurposing of the learning portfolio is already under way, particularly the use of e-portfolios in colleges, CAEL expects such uses to become much more common and move with the individual after graduation into the workplace. In addition, as making connections to the workplace becomes more important, the e-portfolio will, CAEL believes, evolve to more effectively meet employer needs, such as making stronger connections between the individual's portfolio and industry-defined competencies.

Issues and Questions

The potential uses of PLA are indeed exciting for the future of higher education, workforce development, and talent management. Yet thinking about these new opportunities for repurposing PLA raises several important issues and questions. Two issues that are front and center are faculty support and financial aid.

Faculty Support. In the 1970s and 1980s, CAEL recognized that PLA would gain acceptance within the academy only if the faculty knew more about the rationale for the process, the learning theory that supports it, and the academic integrity and rigor of PLA methods. To address many of these issues, CAEL articulated 10 standards to ensure academic quality of the assessments, regardless of the format. Even today, these standards are accepted by the six regional accreditors and are practiced by all reputable PLA practitioners (see Fiddler, Marienau, & Whitaker, 2006).

Since 1974, CAEL has trained thousands of faculty members across the country. This training has helped PLA take root and flourish, particularly within adult learning programs. Yet the faculty members whom CAEL trained 30 years ago are now nearing or have already reached retirement age. The new generation of faculty often does not have the same background and training in PLA but has the potential to bring fresh ideas to the use of PLA within institutions. Thus, a new round of faculty development would help new academics support the value of PLA and put their own imprint on it.

Financial Aid. Currently federal financial aid through loans and grants (e.g., Pell grants) supports traditional time-based, credit-hour-based learning, whether such learning is in the classroom or online. In addition, Section 127 employer-provided educational assistance programs, veteran education benefits (e.g., GI Bill education benefits), and Individual Training Accounts through the Workforce Investment Act either do not allow or are unclear about whether assessments of learning are an allowable expense. CAEL is working to educate the federal government about PLA and to ask for policy changes that allow Title IV funding to cover all costs associated with assessing students' college-level knowledge, skills, and abilities for the purposes of awarding college credit or granting advanced standing.

There are additional questions to consider as well, specifically in regard to terminology. What do we call this area now? The examples of expanded uses of PLA methods call into question the term *prior learning assessment*. In some cases, such as MOOCs, it is not so much prior learning or experiential learning that is to be assessed but rather *current* learning that takes place through an alternative delivery system. Yet, using a more generic term like *learning assessment* does not capture the underlying message regarding the assessment and valuing of learning that happens outside a postsecondary institution. CAEL believes that finding the right terminology could be an important step in promoting greater use and acceptance of PLA.

Conclusion

The postsecondary landscape is changing rapidly. On what seems to be a daily basis, educators, critics, and the media call attention to the urgency of degree completion and the impact of competency-based assessments, OERs, MOOCs, badges, the high cost of education, dwindling public resources, and the social and economic imperatives of expanding educational opportunities. Addressing these issues—and others that will emerge in the 21st century—effectively will surely require many creative, sometimes complex approaches. Some of these strategies will be entirely new; others will involve new applications of approaches that have already been shown to be effective. And one of the latter is PLA. Of course, PLA alone cannot provide an answer to all of the conundrums facing students, institutions, employers, and the public sector. Yet it is an important tool in our toolkit. Indeed, the possibilities for expanding the uses of PLA are without limit.

References

Fiddler, M., Marienau, C., & Whitaker, U. (Eds.). (2006). *Assessing learning: Standards, principles & procedures*, 2nd ed. Chicago, IL: Council for Adult & Experiential Learning.

Hossler, D., Shapiro, D., Dundar, A., Ziskin, M., Chen, J., Zerquera, D., & Torres, V. (2012, February). *Transfer & mobility: A national view of pre-degree student movement in postsecondary institutions*. Herndon, VA: National Student Clearinghouse Research Center. Retrieved from http://nscresearchcenter.org/wp-content/uploads/NSC_Signature_Report_2.pdf

Klein-Collins, R. (2010). *Fueling the race to postsecondary success: A 48-institution study of prior learning assessment and adult student outcomes*. Chicago, IL: Council for Adult and Experiential Learning. Retrieved from http://www.cael.org/pdfs/PLA_Fueling-the-Race

Klein-Collins, R. (2012). *Competency-based degree programs in the U.S.: Postsecondary credentials for measurable student learning and performance*. Chicago, IL: Council for Adult & Experiential Learning.

Laitinen, A. (2012, September). Cracking the credit hour. *New America Foundation*. Retrieved from http://newamerica.net/publications/policy/cracking_the_credit_hour

Lederman, D. (2013, February 7). Expanding pathways to MOOC Credit. *Inside Higher Ed*. Retrieved from http://www.insidehighered.com/news/2013/02/07/ace-deems-5-massive-open-courses-worthy-credit

Lumina Foundation. (2011). *The degree qualifications profile: Defining degrees: A new direction for American higher education to be tested and developed in partnership with faculty, students, leaders, and stakeholders*. Indianapolis, IN: Author. Retrieved from http://www.luminafoundation.org/publications/The_Degree_Qualifications_Profile.pdf

The Mozilla Foundation and Peer 2 Peer University. (2012, August 27). *Open badges for lifelong learning: Exploring an open badge ecosystem to support skill development and lifelong learning for real results such as jobs and advancement* [Working document]. In collaboration with The MacArthur Foundation. Retrieved from https://wiki.mozilla.org/images/5/59/OpenBadges-Working-Paper_012312.pdf

National Commission on Higher Education Attainment. (2013, January 23). *An open letter to college and university leaders: College completion must be our priority*. Retrieved from http://www.acenet.edu/news-room/Pages/An-Open-Letter-to-College-and-University-Leaders.aspx

Sherman, A., Klein-Collins, B., & Palmer, I. (2012). *State policy approaches to support prior learning assessment: A resource guide for state leaders*. Chicago, IL: Council for Adult and Experiential Learning and HCM. Retrieved from http://www.cael.org/pdfs/College-Productivity-Resource-Guide2012

U.S. Department of Labor. (2010, December 15). *Training and employment guidance letter (TEGL) 15–10*. Retrieved from http://wdr.doleta.gov/directives/attach/TEGL15-10.pdf

U.S. Department of Labor. (2013, April 19). *Notice of availability of funds and solicitation for grant applications for Trade Adjustment Assistance Community College and Career Training grants program. SGA/DFA Py-12-10*. Retrieved from http://www.doleta.gov/grants/pdf/taaccct_sga_dfa_py_12_10.pdf

REBECCA KLEIN-COLLINS, MPP, *is the director of research for the Council for Adult and Experiential Learning (CAEL).*

JUDITH B. WERTHEIM, EdD, *is the vice president for higher education services for CAEL.*

6

Noncredit programs help to define continuing education programs. Current trends indicate that change in noncredit programming will continue, and likely accelerate, as a result of new audiences, technologies, and institutional expectations.

Trends and Considerations Affecting Noncredit Programs

Nelson C. Baker

Introduction

Programs offered by continuing education (CE) units define who they are and the engagements they have with their many stakeholders. While shifts are evident in the landscape of CE programs, both by design and from external forces, few could dispute that higher education is changing and consequently so are CE units and programs. Historically, CE units at many universities have been the entrepreneurs and experimenters, the people who created new programs, technologies, and partnerships between the campus and the community. In today's climate, these programs span diverse audiences, from community service programs to professional certification programs offered locally in face-to-face environments, online, or in a blended format. To reflect a renewed emphasis on professional learning, some programs have added "professional" to their name; in fact, a major national association changed its name from University Continuing Education Association to the University Professional and Continuing Education Association (UPCEA).

Many CE programs now serve audiences beyond their communities, regions, and states, yet not long ago the majority of program enrollees resided within commuting distance of the campus or program location. The role of CE within higher education is also evolving. Programs are expected to provide education beyond traditional audiences, including engaging in workforce development and forging ties to professions and economic development organizations. For some CE units, participating in state attempts to attract new businesses by offering free or low cost training is common.

The role of noncredit programs within universities is also changing. Programs now serve internal stakeholders, faculty, administration, and students as well as external audiences; in research universities, CE programs often participate in dissemination activities and research development or resource cultivation—CE instructors are finding new research opportunities as they teach to external audiences, often in industry and government.

The types of noncredit programs offered by CE units are very diverse, spanning the spectrum from precollegiate programs for high school students, to learning for personal enjoyment, professional advancement, and certification, contract programs for employers, economic development initiatives, and initiatives targeted to specific population groups, such as the Lifelong Learning Institutes funded by the Bernard Osher Foundation (2012) for seniors. The particular mix of noncredit programs is a function of the institutional mission as well as the particular CE unit's mission and programming history.

As the landscape of higher education evolves, new programs and delivery modalities are also spawned; examples include free classes and massive open online courses (MOOCs) with enrollments in the thousands. The rationale for the changes may be rooted in educational reform as well as the globalization and needs of people, organizations, and communities (Walshok, 2012).

In this changing context, what is the role of CE programs? What are the latest trends, who are programs serving, for what reasons do stakeholders engage with programs? The answers will determine a CE unit's course of action and its program offerings. This discussion of CE programs includes the audience(s) and the credentials CE provides, types of programs designed to meet the audiences/stakeholders' needs, and business models and best practices that make these programs successful. Finally, some thoughts on future trends are presented.

Multiple Stakeholders for CE Programs

In a broad sense, stakeholders for CE programs can be grouped into three categories: the learners, the campus structure in which the CE unit is located, and the general public.

Learners who enroll in noncredit programs typically fall into a variety of categories, including the general public, alumni, members of specific professions, and employees of businesses or government agencies that contract with CE units to provide training. These categories suggest that CE programs serve populations sometimes described as K to gray, from precollege to post–high school and extending well into retirement. Therefore, programs have commitments to serve both specific geographic communities as well as communities of focused audiences of individuals and organizations that may be local or international. These communities span the generations and often are found in a single class or program, thus causing interesting learning dynamics and preferences where many learning styles must be addressed.

A program's learners come with many aspirations; some come for the joy of learning something new while others come to update job-related knowledge and skills, professional certifications to remain employed, and the skills to find new employment or careers. To satisfy these multiple program objectives and learner goals, programs also must offer student services, sometimes in locations beyond their own campuses. The presence or absence of these services (e.g., adult learning support, after-hours technology support, career advising) often determines whether a program will be successful or fail.

The second stakeholder group is the internal customer, including instructors, campus administrators to whom CE programs report, and the organizational governance structures CE organizations often must navigate. Governance structures can have a significant impact on CE programs, especially in how quickly they can address new market trends and how amendable they are to change and adaptability and to the processes needed to eliminate outdated programs. If CE programs can be aligned to meet internal customers' expectations initially, the unit will be better positioned to thrive and prosper.

Understanding the university mission is critical for program success. When programs are offered that are outside the public's perception of the university, success can be difficult to achieve. Further, understanding institutional hiring practices and the constraints faced when hiring instructors who are not "regular" faculty impacts the operation of the programs and their potential for success. Some programs, such as those to promote economic and workforce development, may be feeder programs into more traditional academic programs and typically must satisfy constituencies beyond an individual CE unit. In addition, sometimes benefits can be derived when creating programs that align with other campus units. For example, participants of noncredit programs may help to develop new networks and contacts for faculty teaching in the program, including potential research sponsorships.

The third group of stakeholders is the general public, a group that is typically more significant at public universities. CE units should be conscious of the influence that can be harnessed by the public in support of or in opposition to programs being offered. Of obvious influence are the economic conditions in the geographic area in which the campus or extension site is located. In good times, enrollments may be higher, but in lean times, registration may suffer, which affects the program's financial status. Understanding these external factors is crucial to successful programs. Increasingly, a global perspective is desirable for a CE unit as new opportunities are developed abroad. External factors can change the dynamics of enrollment patterns and needs of stakeholders worldwide almost overnight. Of course, these factors also bring opportunities to those who can quickly recognize these dynamics and modify program offerings to exploit them.

There are also policy-level discussions taking place that affect the credentials offered by CE programs. These include articulation agreements between the university provider for noncredit certificate programs and the home institution (University System of Georgia, 2012), to accreditation of nondegree and noncredit programs in the European Union (Lapiner, 2012), to regulatory aspects of taxation, licenses, and approvals both within the United States and overseas.

The regulatory aspects can become very challenging and complicated when working outside of a program's home country, and unwelcome developments, such as a foreign tax, must be avoided when considering international programs.

Program Considerations

Programs offered by CE enterprises must take into account the context and stakeholders previously discussed. The program's business models are also often as important, or more so, than program content. The types of programs offered by a CE unit are typically tied to the unit's mission; thus, they are unlikely to target all potential audiences.

However, there are several practices that CE units often incorporate to maximize program success. These are:

- Program blending
- Outcome design
- Market segments
- Course delivery
- Partnering
- Business model
- Assessment

Program Blending. A single course or educational module that can be used in more than one program can help to increase enrollment and spread development and marketing costs among several programs. Learners may also discover new interests as a result of shared module content.

Outcome Design. From inception, programs are designed to render specific outcomes and to assess learner attainment of course objectives. Results of assessments are used to modify and enhance course content and instruction to improve student learning.

Market Segments. The attempt to reach desired market segments drives course creation and involves learning objectives, content, and delivery. If participants see the content as too superficial, an unfocused program that seeks to attract a broad cross-section of learners might fail due to low enrollment.

Course Delivery. Developing materials specifically for the delivery modality to be used for the intended audience is critical for program success. Often programs delivered face-to-face are copied to an online format, not factoring in the differences between the formats, and the course suffers. Online and face-to-face, or blended, delivery must be designed to enhance the student's ability to reach the learning objectives using the best pedagogical approaches tailored to the unique program and delivery mechanisms. While much content can be utilized in multiple delivery formats, saving time researching and creating materials appropriate to the audience, the particular characteristics of each delivery mode must be considered.

Partnering. Some CE units are finding that partnering with other providers presents opportunities to leverage their own resources and to reach a larger audience than either of the partners could individually attract. Shared development also can result in unique programs that otherwise would be impossible to offer due to budgetary limitations.

Business Model. A key attribute for any CE program is its business and operational model. Although there are a variety of models, all must consider these issues in order to provide a feedback loop for continuous program improvement: (1) identification of subject matter; (2) identification and selection of subject matter experts who will be the pool of potential instructors and program advisors; (3) creation of learning objectives to satisfy the identified objectives; (4) selection of delivery format(s); (5) organization and creation of learning materials; (6) course enrollment management and implementation; and (7) assessment of both the course itself and learner achievement of the stated objectives.

Considerations must be included in the business models for determining course expenses and tuition, either through direct charges (credit card, purchase orders, company contracts) or through financial aid (scholarships, private loans, workforce investment act grants, Veteran Affairs funding, GI bill funding). Some of these payment methods require coordination with appropriate off-campus entities as well as campus business offices and campus policies. These payment options also may differ if the course is designed for open enrollment or as a result of a contract or other external sponsor. Sponsored offerings arise when entities indicate they wish to have a program for their employees or organization and sign a contract for the creation/delivery of the program. Often these offerings are combinations of existing face-to-face courses customized to address the sponsoring organization's specific training goals. However, they also may be completely new programs requiring development from scratch.

Business models also are very different when partnering with other providers. Agreements between the partners typically reflect each party's responsibilities for performing services under the collaborative arrangement and with revenue-sharing models. Significant cost savings sometimes can be realized, but there also needs to be an understanding regarding how program costs, expected and otherwise, will be shared. Partnering agreements also typically address which entity maintains records of program participation and credentials earned as well as policies on credit for prior learning and course articulation agreements (University System of Georgia, 2012). Partnership agreements with external organizations—for example, whereby learners can obtain free content via MOOCs—are evolving. How new business models emerge from these activities will determine how this "free learning" is credentialed and likely will change how some CE programs operate.

Assessment. Programs utilize a variety of assessment tools in determining program quality. Typically there are both formative and summative assessments of learning, evaluation surveys of learning satisfaction, internal and external advisory boards, and direct focus group sessions with former students to understand how the programs affect learners. With such information in hand, instructional designers work with faculty to constantly improve the learners' educational experience. Support infrastructure is refined to address the learners' needs for maximum program and student success. At least one professional organization, the International Association for Continuing Engineering Education (IACEE), is seeking ways globally to document, benchmark, and share lessons learned among CE organizations, with nearly 75 organizations currently participating (IACEE, 2012; Scalzo, Borbely, & Baker, 2012).

Future Trends

With the many changes taking place both inside and outside of higher education, the roles of CE units and their programs can positively impact the lives of many people, create and save jobs, and help increase the number of educated people. What trends may be coming to noncredit continuing education? Potential areas will be outgrowths and solutions to the situations described earlier as well as others, resulting in new endeavors and program models as CE continues to be the incubator of visionary ideas.

Trying to predict the future is always risky and often incorrect, but here are some notable trends.

New Programs. With the changes taking place in the fields of science, technology, engineering, and mathematics (STEM) and with information technology's impact on entire sectors of business and social communication, new types of programming opportunities will continue to emerge. CE units that can sift through data trends and listen carefully to their stakeholders will be able to create new content and learning models. For example, trends in health care will require workers trained in applying information technology to medical records and in-home care technicians who can utilize robotic or telepresence technologies, which enable individuals to remain in their own homes. Other new program ideas come by listening to industry's needs to employ creative problem solvers at all levels of their organizations. CE units that can respond to needs such as these will be more successful and even able to predict future trends.

New Business Models. Free content available via online sources such as YouTube and MOOCs will enable enormous amounts of data to be gathered from the mining of these sites, creating new knowledge on how people learn. The advent of MOOCs provides momentous, expanded opportunities for people to learn in huge numbers; however, there is a real cost to providers who offer content in these formats. Therefore, new business models and forms of revenue generation must be created to cover these costs. Whether it is through licensing the content to create royalties or identifying the most effective learning styles of employees of a given firm, it is clear that the free content will not be sustained without generating supporting revenues.

More Technology Utilization. New technologies will impact significantly how programs are delivered and how learners interact with course materials and one another. From miniaturization of hardware and expansion of storage devices that are driving storage of data and course costs lower, to faster computing cycles, more can be accomplished to support student learning styles. The advent of more reliable and accessible computer networks, coupled with mobile devices, also will change the nature of programs offered and the communication that takes place between participants and instructors. All of these developments will enable more experiential learning activities and, potentially, a global reach for programs.

New Learning Databases. With more individuals requiring professional development and with more providers offering programs, there is an increasing need for some sort of clearinghouse to maintain earned learning credentials allowing learners to go to one location for verification of learning advancement. Many professional groups that require CE of their members do maintain these records, but noncredit CE programs not targeted to a specific profession lack this sort of record keeping on a national level.

Continued Rapid Change. As public pressure for change within higher education accelerates and as for-profit educational companies proliferate, the need for CE units to adapt will only increase. Programs that can adapt to change, diversify offerings, and predict future changes will survive. These same changes might also cause some programs to lose market relevancy and eventually close.

Constant Organizational Change. With the expectation of new programs, new business models, and continued change, it is highly likely that the organizational structures to develop and deploy these educational paradigms also will continue to evolve in a never-ending attempt to meet the needs of the multiple stakeholders involved. The benefits of predictive analysis and data mining of CE enrollments will yield new business, and thus new types of professionals will be required in CE entities. Also, tighter integration with traditional academic programs, processes, and operations of the university will take place, leveraging the efficiencies that CE units have developed in their activities, enabling similar efficiencies campuswide.

Summary

CE units have been and will continue to be defined by the programs they offer to their learners. CE programs will likely become a greater component of the entire university infrastructure, creating new value for the academy. The programs that have been and will be created will continue to be influenced by the many external influences affecting the CE unit as well as driven by the availability of internal resources and competencies. Aligning with the larger university mission will be critical to the future CE unit in meeting the needs of current and future stakeholders. Finally, those who can accept, adapt to, and predict changes will become the CE leaders within their university and for the stakeholders they serve.

References

Bernard Osher Foundation. (2012). *Osher Lifelong Learning Institutes*. Retrieved from http://www.osherfoundation.org/index.php?olli

International Association for Continuing Engineering Education. (2012, May). *The IACEE quality program*. Retrieved from http://www.iacee.org/iacee_quality_program.php

Lapiner, R. S. (2012, July 27). News from Europe: Continuing higher education as a core mission. *The EvoLLLution*. Retrieved from http://www.evolllution.com/opinions/news-from-europe-continuing-higher-education-as-a-core-mission/

Scalzo, K., Borbely, E., & Baker, N. (2012). *Quality standards for continuing professional development organizations and quality management through self-assessment and benchmarking*. American Society for Engineering Education, Paper AC 2012-5363. Retrieved from http://www.iacee.org/docs/Scalzo_Borbely_Baker_ASEE_2012_PAPER.pdf

University System of Georgia. (2012). *Policy and procedures manual: Utilization of the continuing education unit (CEU) within the university system of Georgia*. Athens, GA: Regents Administrative Committee on Public Service and Continuing Education. Retrieved from http://www.usg.edu/docs/Continuing_Education_Policy_and_Procedures_Manual_rev04262012.pdf

Walshok, M. L. (2012). Reinventing continuing higher education. *Continuing Higher Education Review, 76*, 38–53.

NELSON C. BAKER, PhD, is the dean of professional education at the Georgia Institute of Technology.

This chapter expands on the role of community colleges in economic development, workforce development and training, and even job creation. Practical examples from the field are included.

Role of the Community College in Economic Development

Rebecca A. Nickoli

More and more, community colleges are viewed as the engine of economic development for companies that are making plans to relocate and are interested in growing a larger workforce and in training the existing workforce so there is a pipeline of skilled workers ready to step in without lengthy training necessary. Community colleges are achieving a growing recognition at the national level, in part due to the work of Dr. Jill Biden, a successful and dedicated community college professor. Her husband, Vice President Joe Biden, is part of the national administration demonstrating an increased understanding of the role of community colleges in economic development (Flannery, 2012). The community college capacity-building and training grants first made available in 2011 through the U.S. Department of Labor also reflect the understanding that community colleges are increasingly the partner of choice for companies wishing to relocate, expand their existing operations, or train incumbent workers. The grants were authorized in 2009 in the American Recovery and Reinvestment Act (ARRA), which amended the Trade Act of 1974. The Health Care and Education Reconciliation Act of 2010 authorized funding for the grants.

In addition, local economic development organizations (LEDOs) are acknowledging that the community college is an appropriate partner to bring to the table when courting new business or convincing a business not to leave the area. LEDOs are entities that work on behalf of a community or region to attract new businesses or keep current businesses in the area. They often work with other local partners to create incentives for businesses or sell the area's assets to prospective businesses.

Community colleges can identify recent program graduates in discipline areas being sought by a new company; identify for-credit students currently in the educational pipeline; and recommend continuing education (CE) students who have taken short-term training from the college to update skills or acquire new certifications. They also can provide services that include assessing the skills of job candidates; training those potential candidates to give them the skills they need before they start a new job; training for incumbent workers to "upskill" them for new, more technical, and more complex jobs; and training for dislocated workers who formerly operated in lower-skilled positions that are no longer available. In the community college, the function of adult continuing education may be administratively placed in a workforce development or "corporate college" department as continuing education may address education that is more professional and technical in nature in addition to the kinds of training mentioned previously.

There are many examples of community partnerships, but there is still some frustration that community colleges are not always at the table when LEDOs are discussing what variables must be part of a package that will keep an important company in the community or attract a new one. Stereotypes about what kinds of training or services community colleges can provide often exist, so these institutions may be invited only when businesses are being recruited that have workers needing those skills—for example, machining fundamentals or welding. Community college workforce departments are more sophisticated than external agencies may recognize, as evidenced by their ability to understand complex business problems and work together with businesses on creative solutions.

Community colleges provide training across a wide variety of discipline areas, including leadership and supervision, soft skills, quality and safety courses, language and culture, mathematics and writing skills development, and more. In addition, college workforce and economic development departments also provide services such as job profiling, assessment of prospective job candidates or incumbent workers, and developing training that matches the skills gap. Many adults in the workforce along with dislocated workers affected by layoffs, company closures, and salary increases do not demonstrate the high level of skills expected by employers and thus can benefit from the courses and programs offered by CE and/or workforce departments.

This chapter discusses the ways in which partnering is occurring within the community with multiple organizations, including K–12 education, colleges, chambers of commerce, and LEDOs, and ways in which community colleges have become respected and sought-after partners by economic development stakeholders.

Community college representatives should ensure that the college is present on boards that routinely assess and develop strategies regarding the local business climate so they can best understand the strategies that are in place to attract and retain business and industry and be part of crafting those strategies. The ongoing participation of the college can help it forecast what new programs (both for-credit programming and short-term training) it might need to develop to support the goals for job creation. Local college representatives can participate in business advance teams who go to the corporate headquarters of a company that is looking for new expansion sites or to relocate.

Workforce Training or Economic Development?

Most community colleges have departments that address workforce training, offered both to individuals and to companies. Training may be offered through open enrollment scheduling to adults who are seeking skills enhancement in order to find new employment or advance at a current employer. In many cases, small or medium-size employers may seek training for their workers but cannot accumulate the critical mass of employees who need the same training. Further, small employers may not have many training dollars available and so send workers to courses that are open to the public at the community college. *Customized training* refers to new training developed either at the company's specific request or adapted from an off-the-shelf course to solve the business problem identified by the company, whether it is employee turnover, waste, safety, or any number of other issues the company hopes to resolve through employee training.

How is economic development, as experienced in the community college environment, different from simply providing workforce training? At the most basic level, economic development involves the attraction of new businesses and the retention and/or expansion of existing ones. The role of the community college in economic development may involve several approaches. One approach occurs when the area's business environment is simply not generating enough jobs to sustain the population in that community. As a result, the out-migration of workers who believe they must leave in order to find jobs with family-sustaining wages may occur. Or a higher unemployment rate may occur if workers cannot afford to relocate for new jobs due to their financial situation, as in the recent downturn in housing sales and high rates of foreclosure. Thus, the community college is responsible, through its traditional mission of creating a local skilled workforce by serving students of all ages and all levels of academic preparation, for helping to build a pipeline of workers to serve not only current needs but to prepare workers for future anticipated jobs.

The forecasting and timing of filling that pipeline are challenges that must involve the community and its business and economic development leaders. Some colleges and community entities are using "job scraping" technologies, which automate the process of scanning job postings in large Web sites (such as Monster.com) to look for key words and phrases that they have in common (Bradley, 2011). Data vary by regional economies, but the trend is that more jobs will require more than high school preparation but less than a bachelor's degree. Thus, the credentials offered by the community colleges to the workplace become even more important—the associate degree, the one-year certificates and other short-term training, especially that which results in a nationally recognized, third-party, portable credential. More colleges are building career pathways or career ladders that allow students/workers to exit and reenter educational programs at multiple points and earn multiple credentials on their way to an associate degree or beyond (Conway, Blair, & Helmer, 2012).

Examples from the Field

The author interviewed several colleagues from across the country, looking for economic development examples from community colleges small and large, rural and urban.

An Arkansas Partnership. While many examples of economic development partnerships involve attracting new business to local communities, Jo Blondin, chancellor, and Ken Warden, chief business and community outreach officer, at Arkansas Tech University–Ozark Campus (ATU-Ozark) agree that other partnerships focus on keeping existing businesses or helping them to expand their operations (personal communication, August 2012). In Arkansas, Green Bay Packaging partnered with ATU–Ozark Campus to create a training collaborative that includes 13 companies overall, funded in part by Green Bay Packaging with some assistance from the Arkansas Department of Workforce Services. The area around the location of the training center in Morrilton, Arkansas, has a population of around 200,000, and the training collaborative serves seven counties along the I-40 corridor from Little Rock to Ozark. Most companies involved engage in traditional manufacturing but with different products, including processed food technology, production of paper products, and energy.

Green Bay Packaging bought an abandoned factory, relocated a portion of its operation there, and remodeled the remainder of the space into a training center. The community college stepped in to assist with curriculum development and training the trainers. Classes are offered on a 6-week, 48 contact-hour rotation; each costs $150. (Contact hours and cost are similar to a three-credit course, although the courses are offered on a not-for-credit basis.) Courses include the basics of electricity, mechanics, and instrumentation, and students range from entry-level workers to engineers. Employees are paid for the hours they spend in class, and some companies have tied promotion and pay increases to course completion.

An Industry Council has been created that operates much like a program advisory committee. It provides insights and advice about how current classes are going and what should be next on the menu of training topics.

Ms. Blondin and Mr. Warden reported that, although the training center now serves a total of 13 companies, early on there were the typical company fears of poaching promising workers from each other and sharing too much about internal operations. However, with time has come trust, and workers interact to create synergy around solving workplace problems in the classroom; the value of the training has overridden the earlier concerns. Some students even act as peer mentors to others. The training collaborative started operation in 2009 and recently increased participation; between January and August 2012, over 300 workers had completed training at the facility, and momentum around this project continues to grow.

Gary Sams, of Green Bay Packaging Inc., Arkansas Kraft Division, said:

> The level of hands-on skills and the multitude of topics needed by industry today are not available in standard two-year community college course offerings. In 2009, when the Training Center opened, and still today, this is the only training center of this nature and magnitude operating in our region. Green Bay Packaging and ATU-Ozark share a common vision of what needs to be accomplished, understand what's at stake, and the consequences of doing nothing. (Reported by Mr. Warden in personal communication, August 2012)

Macomb Community College. According to James Sawyer, provost and vice president for the Learning Unit at Macomb Community College in Warren, Michigan, the school has long been considered a strong partner in economic development in Macomb County (personal communication, September 2012). Macomb is invited to the table when economic development conversations are taking place and strategies are being crafted to attract new businesses or help keep current employers. One staff member is a regular member of a countywide economic development group.

The college was a convener for a consortium focused on attracting additional defense business to southeast Michigan. The consortium activities were funded by the New Economy Initiative, part of grant activities financed by 10 philanthropic organizations in Michigan with a focus on workforce and economic development. The New Economy Initiative developed marketing materials to attract attention to the region's resources for defense contractors and spoke with one voice to define and describe those resources. Although the grant itself has ended, the initiative has not. It has been transitioned to an arm of the Michigan Economic Development Council and is now called the Arsenal of Innovation, a reference to the area's designation during World War II as the Arsenal of Democracy.

Mr. Sawyer confirmed that in Michigan, there are 11 Procurement Technical Assistance Centers (PTACs), some situated at colleges and some at chambers of commerce. The PTACs were created in states throughout the country by Congress to assist businesses that wish to compete for federal contracts. The goals of the PTACs are to help small businesses learn about and understand the defense procurement business so they can become approved as suppliers and effectively compete for business. The work of the PTACs was particularly beneficial when the auto industry suffered from the recession that began in 2008, and small suppliers were looking for contracts to replace those they had with automakers. The colleges involved in the PTACs offer their resources in kind. Other funding comes from the Michigan Economic Development Council Corporation along with some federal funding. Another initiative in Michigan, the Southeast Michigan Community College Consortium, received a U.S. Department of Labor grant through which it developed and shared curriculum across colleges that can be used to craft quick responses to industry needs. James Jacobs, Macomb's president, believes that Macomb Community College is an excellent example of how community colleges can be involved in strategy development, partnership development, and the implementation of economic development plans (personal communication, September 2012).

According to President Jacobs, Macomb Community College has also organized and led the Auto Communities Consortium, a group of community colleges that serve regional economies impacted by automotive manufacturing layoffs and closures. The colleges meet regularly to discuss common issues and have collaborated on a grant opportunity that could further consolidate the consortium's efforts to build and share workforce development strategies and new curricula in response to changing needs. The consortium's membership is fluid with as many as 35 colleges participating from across the Midwest, Plains, and southern states. One important element of this consortium is that the member college presidents are fully engaged in the group's activities.

Harper College. According to Maria Coons, senior executive to the president and executive director for workforce and strategic alliances, Harper College in Palatine, Illinois, is widely recognized for engaging local business and industry partners in developing programs and curricula that meet local needs (personal communication, September 2012). Harper's district is located near O'Hare International Airport and several major highways and distribution centers, making the area a manufacturing and logistics hub for northern Illinois. More than 25 manufacturers participated in a forum Harper officials recently held to discuss the challenges employers are having in finding qualified employees. Some explained that the lack of qualified workers prompted them to turn down orders, impeding the growth of their companies. Two key participants, Acme Industries, a precision machining operation located in Elk Grove Village, and Nation Pizza and Foods, a food manufacturer located in Schaumburg, exemplify the diversity of manufacturing in the area. Although the type of manufacturing in which they are engaged varies, these companies are experiencing the same workforce challenges. As a result of the forum, a manufacturing task force was formed that includes these industry partners, local high schools, local workforce development offices (sometimes colloquially called the unemployment office), veterans' organizations, and trade associations. All participated in the development of the program and recruitment of students.

According to Ms. Coons, the result of the collaboration is the development of a new program in advanced manufacturing underpinned by nationally recognized Manufacturing Skills Standards Council (MSSC) certifications, available in production and logistics, technical mathematics, and an internship. The internship, which involves a paid work experience at the conclusion of the first basic certificate, is the centerpiece of the program. Harper's goal was to secure 50 internships with area employers; instead, over 90 came to fruition. This underscores the commitment by area manufacturers to not only provide paid work experiences but to nurture students' interests in this career field. Subsequent certificates are stacked in various manufacturing specialties including welding, computerized numerical control (CNC), and mechatronics. The courses are offered for college credit so eligible students can receive Title IV financial aid. The stacked certificates also provide a pathway to an associate's degree in advanced manufacturing; thus, once employed, students may be able to use employer tuition reimbursement programs to continue their studies. This Earn and Learn program has been nominated for an Illinois Community College Innovation Award.

Ivy Tech Community College. Ivy Tech Community College, Indiana's statewide community college, has worked closely with Navistar and the United Auto Workers (UAW) to redefine and restart a closed manufacturing plant on the east side of Indianapolis. When the large Navistar plant closed in 2008, the community college, with the local workforce development entity as a strong partner, worked with the company to upgrade the skills of many workers who were dislocated and looking for other employment in manufacturing. Basic computer training was offered to hundreds, and many others received CNC training. Due to the closure of other local companies in the same time period, small service-oriented businesses closed as well, and many buildings were left vacant.

Sue G. Smith, corporate executive for manufacturing and technology at Ivy Tech, said that both the UAW and Navistar management had a vision for reopening the location with a new brand, but one that needed much more highly skilled workers (personal communication, September 2012). With Navistar as its parent company, Pure Power Technology (PPT) was developed. PPT uses compacted graphite iron to make engine blocks, the only such technology company in the United States. PPT opened in 2011, hiring back many of the former Navistar employees who were willing to undergo training for the new, high-tech facility. Again, the community college provided the training.

PPT has proven to be a leader in revitalizing the entire neighborhood, called the Irvington Innovation Zone. PPT, the city of Indianapolis, other business partners including Kroger, and the community college are seeking grants to help find tenants for the numerous vacant buildings in the Irvington neighborhood.

Ivy Tech Community College was there for the Navistar plant closure, the interim period of retraining workers, and the birth of PPT, helping to bring new life to a company and its employees and to a neighborhood.

Entrepreneurship and the Community College

In recent years, community colleges have become much more involved in entrepreneurship. They are hosting business incubators and assisting students and small-business people to set up and maintain successful business practices.

Virtual Incubation Network Toolkit. According to Jennifer Worth, program manager for the Center for Workforce and Economic Development for the American Association of Community Colleges (AACC), the organization has recently developed the Virtual Incubation Network (VIN) Toolkit for community colleges to implement locally (American Association of Community Colleges, n.d.). Eleven community colleges from around the country were instrumental in the development of the VIN, which is framed around serving three basic client types: the entrepreneurial student, the existing small-business owner, and the new small-business start-up. The VIN identifies resources that the community college can assist with, such as: networking events, inventor councils, coaching and mentoring from successful business owners or retiree groups, referrals to agencies such as the Small Business Development Council, and access to financial institutions that provide small business loans. In addition, some community colleges provide incubation space for student entrepreneurs and other small-business start-ups. The space may come with shared services available to its tenants, such as marketing, accounting, and information technology support.

Kingsborough Community College. Babette Audant, director of the Center for Economic and Workforce Development at Kingsborough Community College in New York, explained that the area is dominated by small businesses. Thus, the community college offers programs and support for entrepreneurial opportunities (personal communication, September 2012). The college has, for example, an incubator for small food-service businesses. Numerous rooftop garden businesses in New York have begun serving local restaurants and grocery produce departments, and these garden businesses can get support from the community college. The college has recently started working more closely with the Brooklyn Economic Development Council, which has offices on the campus. Serving small businesses can be difficult, as they often do not have the money to pay for short-term training or credit courses for their employees. Thus, colleges serving small businesses must find grant opportunities to help them provide such services.

Special Challenges of Rural Colleges

When talking with industry leaders around the country, the author learned that the challenge to become involved in economic development activities can be very different between small and large colleges and between rural and urban colleges.

Colleges and others involved in economic development must be sensitive to the very personal rural ethos, wherein individuals who meet at the economic development table are the same ones who meet on other important community issues, at their children's schools, at church, and at the Friday night high school football games. This ongoing interconnectedness underpins people's ability to work collaboratively on issues and to have a tacit understanding of the value of the work of attracting new businesses and keeping current ones. In addition, community college representatives may need to drive long distances to tend to economic and workforce development relationships in such areas, as small towns (even though distant from one another) are often part of regional economies and work closely together to attract business to a region rather than focusing only on a single small town.

White Mountains Community College. John Dyer, director of community and corporate affairs at White Mountains Community College in New Hampshire, explained that the college is an example of a small college in a rural area that remains very involved in economic development activities (personal communication, August 2012). He shared information about the Northern Forest Sustainable Economy Initiative (SEI), which involves New Hampshire, Maine, Vermont, and northern New York that have joined together to "reinvigorate the rural economies of the Northern Forest" (Northern Forest Sustainable Economy Initiative, 2008, para. 1).The Northern Forest Lands Council 10th Anniversary Forum report instigated the collaborative activity and studied forest products, utilities, banking, education, arts, the environment, and tourism. Leaders from the four states appointed to the study group developed a shared vision that includes: protecting and enhancing the region's assets; expanding enterprise by encouraging workforce, entrepreneurial, and business development; and coordinating and advocating for development as a region.

Summary and Conclusion

Community colleges must be proactive in presenting themselves as partners in economic development. They must partner more aggressively with universities, K–12 schools, local economic development entities, chambers of commerce, and other community organizations committed to building sustainable and vibrant local and regional economies. In some cases, community colleges actually can contribute to job creation by training entrepreneurs who can then grow more successful businesses with an expanding employee base. The colleges can work in advance of newly forming technologies, such as electric vehicles or SmartGrid technology, and create the trained workforce that will help to attract new businesses. Growing a talented local workforce can encourage already established businesses to convert to new technology, knowing there will be trained employees available to work. More funders have targeted grants and technical assistance to help grow capacity and leadership in the community college so that it may more often become a partner of choice in economic development strategies.

References

American Association of Community Colleges. (n.d.). *Virtual Incubator Network Toolkit (VIN), welcome letter*. Retrieved from http://www.aacc.nche.edu/Resources/aaccprograms/cwed/vintoolkit/Pages/default.aspx

Bradley, H. (2011, May 5). *What is job scraping?* Retrieved June 14, 2013, from www.articleonlinedirectory.com/648946/what-is-job-scraping.html

Conway, M., Blair, A., & Helmer, M. (2012). *Courses to employment: Partnering to create paths to education and careers.* Washington, DC: Aspen Institute, Workforce Strategies Initiative.

Flannery, M. E. (2012, March 26). Interview with Dr. Jill Biden: Community colleges connect the dots. *NEA Today.* Retrieved from http://neatoday.org/2012/03/26/interview-with-jill-biden-community-colleges-connect-the-dots/

Northern Forest Sustainable Economy Initiative. (2008). Sustainability initiative. *Northern Forest Center.* Retrieved from www.northernforest.org/sustainable_economy_initiative_.html

REBECCA A. NICKOLI, EdD, *is the vice president for the Corporate College at Ivy Tech Community College in Indiana and the 2012–2013 president of the National Council on Workforce Education, an affiliated council of the American Association of Community Colleges.*

9

Today's programs and delivery methods in continuing education for the adult student are evolving due to changing needs, competition, and new markets and technologies. The marketing infrastructure, including staffing, budgeting, and processes such as customer relationship marketing and market research, must be in alignment with changing needs.

Preparing Marketing for the Future: Strategic Marketing Challenges for Continuing Education

James Fong

Introduction

Ongoing developments in continuing education (CE) for the adult student are transforming the role of marketing as well as the professionals working within the field. Competitive forces, evolution of electronic marketing technologies, developments in data mining and customer relationship management (CRM), along with the greater expectations of marketing metrics and accountability, are helping to reshape how marketing units are positioned within CE. However, many leaders in CE fail to grasp the complexity of marketing, often seeing it simply as graphic design and copywriting (Fong, 2009). Marketing in this era of CE, as well as within corporate America, requires true marketing skills to address multiple factors: governance (where marketing is in the strategic planning process), how marketing is staffed and organized, what electronic (including social media) and traditional tools marketing is using, how marketing is measuring success and accountability, what marketers are doing to stay abreast of new tools and developments, and how marketers can utilize the vast amount of research and information now available to them. Marketing is no longer just creating brochures and writing press releases. It has become a creative science.

CE deans, from an organizational standpoint, have traditionally viewed marketing as an auxiliary service and relegated it to a support role. Only recently and among the more progressive CE leaders has marketing been valued as a strategic part of the planning process. In 2011, the University

Professional and Continuing Education Association (UPCEA) Center for Research and Consulting (CRC) conducted a management survey of its member institutions, which include over 358 of the leading colleges and universities in North America, to determine the average annual salaries in their CE units over a 5-year period from 2006 to 2011 (UPCEA, 2006, 2007, 2008, 2009, 2011a). In total, 171 institutions participated, a 41% response rate (UPCEA, 2011a). In 2006, marketing leaders were making $45,000, which represented a 5-year high since 2001 (UPCEA, 2006). The survey revealed that by 2011, the average salary of marketing leaders had risen to $70,000, an increase of 56% (UPCEA, 2011a).

Over the same period, compensation for deans or chief executive officers rose from $119,000 to $136,000, a 14% increase. Second-in-command administrators saw their salaries rise 28%, from $72,000 to $92,000. The significantly greater 56% increase for marketers further illustrates their growing value and signals the transformation of the CE marketing function. This gain also surpassed the percentage increases for conference planners, executive education leaders, and e-learning specialists within the units, with only financial directors experiencing a greater jump (UPCEA, 2006, 2007, 2008, 2009, 2011a).

From 2006 to 2011, many CE units were rapidly expanding their distance education programs, and more progressive deans found it necessary to hire more experienced marketers, often from outside higher education (UPCEA, 2006, 2007, 2008, 2009, 2011a). The previous generation of marketers had degrees in graphic design, public relations, or communications; the new marketers possessed different credentials such as a degree in digital media or technology or an MBA and were well grounded in integrated marketing strategies, positioning, competition, data-driven strategies, and market research as well as electronic marketing. However, many other CE units maintained their marketing infrastructures and staffing, often choosing to transform existing staff rather than hiring people with MBAs from outside higher education.

Problems existed for both groups of marketing leaders. Many new marketers brought in from the outside found adapting to a higher education culture exceptionally challenging, as it was overly bureaucratic and slow to make decisions. While these marketers had the skills necessary for the evolving competitive era, they often lacked appreciation or patience for the traditional collaborative decision-making processes in higher education. Veteran CE marketers who were asked to reengineer their skills often did not have the time or ability to learn new marketing tools as quickly as necessary (Fong, 2009).

Further compounding problems for both marketers new to higher education and those transforming their skill sets was that few deans could provide them with appropriate leadership and mentoring as they themselves lacked marketing knowledge, expertise, and knowledge about what their future marketing needs might be. Ultimately, deans and marketing directors cited major differences in perceived performance, with the latter awarding themselves

Figure 1. Rating of Marketers by Deans and Marketing Leaders.

	Strategic Marketing Planning	Customer Relationship Management	Market Research	Use of Metrics and Measures
Deans	2.45	2.63	2.33	2.22
Marketing Leaders	3.68	3.29	3.1	3

Source: Fong (2009).

higher performance marks in four categories evaluated in a recent UPCEA marketing survey. Grading was on a 5-point scale, and deans rated performance on average at 2.41 while marketers gave an average score of 3.27 (Figure 1).

The marketers gave themselves the highest grade (3.68) for strategic marketing planning, over 50% more than deans. The lowest rating by both groups was in the use of metrics and measures: 3.0 by the marketers and 2.22 by the deans. In between, numbers were awarded for CRM (which achieved the highest score from the deans) and market research. Overall, the market leaders rated themselves 36% higher than did deans.

Organizational Structure

Changing organizational structures add further complexity to marketing. UPCEA has witnessed a number of different occurrences and debates regarding which organizational marketing structure for adult students works best and in what situation. In many cases, marketers are asked to evolve their departments from purely creative approaches to more strategic marketing units, as mentioned. These units not only evolve strategically but tactically by adding electronic marketing competencies. Other models that have been considered include marketing responsibilities being central to the greater college or university. The argument for an institutionally centralized marketing department is that it provides greater consistency of brand usage and management or achieves more efficiency through improved media buying power and the ability to cross-market programs. These results are rarely ever achieved, as what usually occurs is a smaller marketing budget or allocated marketing staff resourced to CE programs or a lack of or weakened connection to the adult or corporate learner.

What centralized college or university marketing units often fail to recognize is that marketing to traditional and nontraditional students is vastly different. An analysis as to why students select a particular institution of higher education compiled by Noel-Levitz (2012) reveals that the priorities and preferences differ significantly by student group. For the 55,000 first-year traditional students who participated in the survey, cost, financial aid, and academic reputation were the main priorities followed by campus appearance, geographic setting, and personalized attention. For the 17,000 adult learners surveyed, the priorities were convenience (pacing their coursework and compatibility with their work schedule), academic reputation, and the availability of evening and weekend courses. The marketing implications and the skills needed to market to one group versus the other are vastly different, as is the ability to react quickly to the marketplace and to use different media.

Marketing cannot utilize a cookie-cutter approach that is applied to just any industry. There are important nuances to marketing by industry as well as expertise to be gained by knowing how to market to specific audiences. For example, in the corporate world, there exist business-to-business marketing specialists as well as specialists who understand how to market to the Hispanic population, Asian markets, youth audiences, seniors, and others. Higher education needs to acknowledge that marketing to traditional undergraduate students is different from marketing to alumni, as it would be to adult learners. If the adult or corporate learner market is critical to the institution, then the competencies to reach them must exist strategically within the organization, whether it is in a greater university marketing and communications unit or in a CE division.

Organizational structure and alignment are critical to CE marketing departments. For larger units, it is critical that marketing leaders understand how to organize talent, manage resources, and develop competencies. Also important is to whom marketing staff members report and whether marketing plays a role at the strategic planning level within CE. Marketing leaders and their staffs need to continuously evolve. For marketers new to higher education, understanding the higher education decision-making culture as well as the product they are marketing are both crucial growth areas. For those with a history in higher education, understanding marketing strategy, electronic marketing, and integrating research and information become critical.

There is a need for a higher level of marketing sophistication in order to thrive and survive in the adult student marketplace. The UPCEA marketing survey showed that there is some degree of urgency for marketers to learn more about social media, metrics and analytics, and CRM. Nearly half of marketing respondents felt that professional development to achieve a better understanding of social media was critical (Figure 2). Twenty-five percent listed metrics/analytics/return on investment as next in importance, closely followed by CRM/database management. About 1 in 7 respondents saw a need for search engine optimization expertise, and fewer than 10% considered other varied topics, which included search engine marketing, branding, Web

Figure 2. Marketing Professional Development Interests.

Category	Percentage
Social Media	47%
Metrics/Analytics/Return on Investment	25%
Customer Relationship Management/Database	22%
Search Engine Optimization	14%
Search Engine Marketing/Paid Search	9%
Branding/Strategy/Integrated Marketing	8%
Web Architecture/Content Management	7%
New Technologies	7%
Mobile Communications	5%
Retention/Enrollment Management	5%
E-Mail Marketing	4%
Market Research	4%
Copywriting	3%
Writing Marketing Plans	3%
Traditional Marketing (direct mail, print, etc.)	3%
Other	13%

Source: UPCEA (2011b)

content management, and new technologies. Very little emphasis was placed on e-mail marketing and traditional marketing methods, such as direct mail and print advertising. However, marketers may be pursuing growth and professional development areas in which they are particularly interested or believe to be more critical (UPCEA, 2011b). An external review of marketing trends shows that growth in social media, mobile marketing, and the use of video are increasing but data-driven approaches and market research are becoming more important as baseline skills (eMarketer, 2012).

Organization of the marketing department also needed to evolve and transform. In the 1980s and 1990s, many CE marketing departments were heavily staffed with writers, designers, editors, public relations specialists, and production staff. These were primarily large printing departments, often producing catalogs, flyers, brochures, view books (promotional picture books produced by a college or university to recruit students), and newspaper ads. The evolution from mass media tactics to target marketing in the 1990s and into the 2000s, along with the emergence of many digital technologies, shifted the organizational structure of the CE marketing department. Further accelerating organizational change for the marketing department was the product shift, as many institutions began offering online programs. For the most part, promoting online distance education primarily using print media was often viewed as hypocritical or misdirected, which forced marketing departments to further accelerate their transformation. The results of the 2011 UPCEA (2011b) marketing survey are depicted in Table 1, showing the percentage of

Table 1. Percentage of Marketing Departments with Specific Employees by Size of the Continuing Education Department.

	5 million or less	5.1 million to 15 million	More than 15 million	Total
Marketing director	68%	74%	88%	76%
Marketing associate	52%	44%	88%	56%
E-marketer	34%	33%	68%	44%
Web developer	55%	52%	92%	65%
Graphic designer	55%	52%	84%	63%
Copywriter	34%	19%	72%	40%
Editor	28%	22%	50%	33%
Broadcast	3%	0%	13%	5%
B2B	3%	0%	4%	2%
Media	10%	11%	33%	17%
Market researcher	16%	11%	46%	23%
Public relations	25%	15%	33%	24%
Marketing support	38%	41%	50%	42%
CRM	6%	15%	25%	14%
Call center	0%	4%	17%	6%

Source: UPCEA (2011b)

marketing departments having specific marketing staff, based on gross revenues of the CE unit.

The UPCEA marketing survey also evaluated specific staff designations by size, based on gross revenue, of the CE department. As would be expected, the units exceeding $15 million had the highest percentage in each position. Eighty-eight percent of these units had a marketing director as opposed to 68% at $5 million or less and 74% of those with revenues in the middle. The upper-level institutions also had significantly more marketing associates, e-marketers, Web developers, graphic designers, copywriters, and editors. By 2011, many marketing departments had shifted their organizational focus. Many outsourced copywriting and editing staff. Only larger organizations had market research or media-buying persons on staff.

According to the study, the average marketing department had approximately eight full- or part-time individuals, while larger institutions averaged over 13 (Table 2). Smaller and midsize marketing departments averaged fewer than six and appeared to struggle with being able to support full-time positions in e-marketing, Web development, and market research functions.

The results seem to indicate that marketing resources are also not at adequate levels. The UPCEA survey showed CE departments allocated between 5% and 7% of gross revenue to marketing, which included both salaries of

Table 2. Number of Specific Marketing Staff by Size of the Continuing Education Department.

	5 million or less	5.1 million to 15 million	More than 15 million	Total
Full-time staff	4.40	3.33	11.04	5.89
Part-time staff	1.69	2.07	2.62	2.12
Marketing director	0.91	1.05	1.10	1.02
Marketing associate/manager	0.93	1.23	2.31	1.63
E-marketer	0.55	0.69	1.36	0.96
Web developer	0.91	0.87	1.43	1.12
Graphic designer	1.13	1.28	1.88	1.47
Copywriter	0.79	0.64	1.19	0.98
Editor	0.60	0.78	1.22	0.91
Broadcast	0.10	0.00	0.93	0.73
B2B	0.50	0.00	5.00	2.75
Media	0.20	0.40	0.91	0.65
Market researcher	0.54	0.37	1.60	1.13
Public relations	0.73	0.53	0.89	0.75
Marketing support	0.70	0.75	1.71	1.06
CRM	0.65	0.58	1.23	0.92
Call center	0.00	0.30	5.10	4.14

Source: UPCEA (2011b)

staff and media expenditures. The numbers are significantly lower than calculated previously; surveys of the same population 10 years earlier showed marketing budgets averaging 8% to 12% of gross revenue (Fong, 2004). Institutions with gross revenue of $5 million or less have lower economies of scale and therefore average 11% to 14% of gross revenue allocated to marketing. In order to significantly improve a marketing unit's budget needs, marketing staff will need to show appropriate metrics and return on investment.

Branding and Strategic Positioning

Although there is little research on branding and strategic positioning in continuing education, it is surmised or hypothesized that many marketing efforts are not strategically positioned or differentiated from their competitors. The UPCEA CRC recently conducted a study for an institution of its 12 competitors regarding a specific graduate program offered online. The CRC found that in addition to there being few true competitors offering a similar program online, many colleges and universities failed to communicate their programs or institutional strengths through their Web sites (UPCEA, 2012b).

Likely there are many reasons why institutions have failed to position themselves strategically and differentiate their programs. Some of these may include not having trained marketing leaders to do so or not having baseline information that would dictate a position. Regardless, as marketing departments evolve, these critical skills will be essential in what is expected to be a more competitive environment in the adult student market.

CE marketers, at the least, need to understand when and how to leverage the greater institutional brand and determine whether CE customers, such as adult learners or corporations, value a subbrand of CE. If not, the emphasis should be put on leveraging the primary institutional brand but highlighting the program or degree desired. Some CE units will need to be branded as a destination or place for adult learners to connect. Traditional channels, such as a university's admissions office, may not be welcoming to the unique needs of the adult learner. Thus, the CE department and its subbrand would be important to market.

Role of Information

The underpinning of marketing strategy and positioning (Trout & Ries, 2000) is having good information and intelligence relevant to the marketplace, competition, and market segments (Kotler & Keller, 2011). In today's competitive environment, many institutions have significant information available, including internal inquiry, applicant and student data, and Web analytics. They also have external data sources to consider. UPCEA's marketing survey shows that less than half of the institutions surveyed have an active market research effort, either with internal staff conducting research, tapping into another part of the institution, or outsourcing this function. Without strong market intelligence and research, it is unlikely that a CE unit's marketing can be consistently and strategically delivered (UPCEA, 2011b). For larger CE marketing units, a market research analyst would be an expected position to assist in the new program development, market segmentation, and marketing strategy development. The analyst could also play a major role with CRM, dashboard or performance development, or evaluation and program assessment. The role of market research for smaller institutions could also be essential, if not a competitive advantage. Smaller CE departments could utilize information from a market research process as an equalizer to larger, more resourced competitors.

Marketing units need either in-house staff or outside vendors to conduct market research. Over the last decade, marketing research tools have become more affordable and available to marketing units. Some of these tools include Internet research panels, online survey research design tools, geographic information systems, statistical analysis software, and online demographic and occupational datasets. In addition, many research firms, due in part to intense competition in other industry sectors, have identified education as a stable sector in which to compete. CE associations have seen an increase in market research and consulting firms attending their annual conferences. Roughly one-third of UPCEA marketers state that their CE units have entered into outsourcing relationships with some or many of these providers (UPCEA, 2011b).

Without capable staff, such as a skilled marketing director, manager, or analyst, interpreting marketing research data and creating actions and strategies is very difficult. The UPCEA research also showed that one-third of institutions outsource their market research function. For marketing units, this is the largest percentage of outsourced activities, followed by search engine marketing and Web site development.

CRM systems, such as those offered by companies like Salesforce, Hobsons, and SunGard, have extensive features that allow for marketing departments to better understand their marketing, enrollment, and inquiry conversion efforts. Fewer than half of UPCEA institutions surveyed have an active CRM system (UPCEA, 2011b). Recent interviews of CRM providers and marketing experts by the CRC suggest that many institutions, although they have a system in place, do not actively use the system nor do they have a dashboard, scorecard, or regular reporting metrics (UPCEA, 2013). The research also shows that critical success factors for CRM implementation and management are threefold: (1) having skilled and accountable people; (2) processes, such as how the system is accessed and how performance and conversion metrics are reported; and (3) the technology and how users interface, adapt, and integrate the technology into its processes. CE marketers, in addition to understanding media and strategy, are expected to play a role in integrating CRM processes in the marketing process.

New Media

The genesis of new media adds further complexity to the evolution of the marketing department. It is inevitable that new marketing tools will continue to be developed and become options to the marketer who will have to better understand new methods of communication. Therefore, it will be critical for the marketing department not only to hire intelligent, adaptable marketers but also to invest in their professional development.

Numerous digital marketing techniques have yet to be mastered by many CE marketers who still struggle with e-mail marketing and paid search as well as search engine optimization. These techniques have been available to marketers for the past decade, and their implementation and use have not changed dramatically. One study (Fong, 2010) showed that of 105 institutions researched, few had adequate Web site optimization techniques in place.

As stated, marketers are eager to learn more about social media, which continues to evolve and is considered by many experts as being in its infancy. UPCEA's CRC recently conducted a study for one of its members and interviewed 15 of the leading social media experts in education (UPCEA, 2012a).

These experts felt that the field is changing and will continue to do so and stressed the need for marketers to be more prepared to address social media strategically as opposed to just reacting to new social media gadgets and tools. They underlined the importance of understanding the goals of the organization and the makeup of the target markets and how they use social media. The experts advised that the CE community match organizational goals with social media and target markets only; after doing so should they implement social media tactics and actions.

Although social media sites such as LinkedIn, Facebook, Twitter, and YouTube might be considered mature or at least stable to use as marketing tools, many newer sites at the time of this writing are beginning to have a stronger presence and following, such as Pinterest and FourSquare. However, social media companies are regularly changing the rules, such as Facebook allowing advertisements into its news feed features and introduction of a beta mode search engine tool. Social media as a marketing and communications tool is still in its early stages. CE marketing professionals must understand the social media tools, assign staff to use them as marketing tools, and adapt their marketing budgets to use them.

The CRC expert research (UPCEA, 2012a) also revealed that many CE social media efforts are one-sided, which the experts characterized as not being interactive. These one-sided efforts often consist of uninspiring institutional announcements of financial aid deadlines, admission dates, or speakers coming to campus, and lacked student participation or involvement. Students or potential students were not engaged in social media communication, and it can be hypothesized that they may ultimately disconnect since the one-sided approach is not meaningful. For marketers to be more effective, social media will evolve and become a more critical tool. Marketers will be asked to produce social media plans with specific goals and objectives around increasing the number of "likes," "shares," and referrals, as well as link it to dashboards and other reporting tools.

Developing the Marketer

A CE unit must be aware of the changing technologies and dramatic shifts in the competitive adult student marketplace. This way the CE unit will be best prepared for the future by having the appropriate organizational structure, adequate staffing and budgets, real-time metrics and analytics, and up-to-date CRM and information systems. Most important, however, is having staff members who are constantly improving their skills to match changes in the marketplace. CE departments will have to consider their marketing departments as strategic units and make critical investments in achieving their goals and visions.

The CE unit potentially may have to invest more into the marketing staff than it would other staff members, as the tools and trade of marketing are more likely to change and evolve than those of many other professions. CE marketers are going to need to acquire new skill sets as their field changes and as media shifts. For example, many CE marketers of the 1990s and early 2000s relied heavily on broadcast and print marketing channels. In recent years, newspaper readership has declined significantly with just 49% of adults reading a newspaper regularly (Pew Research Center, 2012), down from a peak of 71% in 1996. Continued shifts from more expensive broadcast media to digital video and radio also will require marketers to retool their skills. Social media is expected to be the next growth area. If CE departments are to keep pace with the competition, staff development of marketers will have to be more strategically planned and effectively budgeted.

Conclusion

The CE marketing department will require significant transformation. The department will have to be aligned with the greater goals of the CE unit, be able to adapt to the changing adult student media preferences, eager to learn new marketing and communication skills, and adapt its budgets to address a more competitive environment. Marketers will need to become active members of CE leadership but still work effectively in the culture of academia. Marketing has become a complex science that requires the professional to adapt to new developments, technologies, and other factors. Marketers will have to straddle the fast pace of competition in the adult learner arena in a changing marketplace while helping to transform the way marketing functions within academia.

References

eMarketer. (2012, October 22). *Growth of average time spent per day with major media.* Retrieved from http://www.emarketer.com/newsroom/index.php/consumers-spending-time-mobile-growth-time-online-slows/
Fong, J. (2004). *The state of continuing education: Five years later.* Presentation at the 2004 University Continuing Education Association National Meeting, San Antonio, TX.
Fong, J. (2009). Improving the relationship between continuing education leadership and marketing directors. *Continuing Higher Education Review, 73,* 153–162.
Fong, J. (2010). *The 2010 review of continuing and distance education websites* [Corporate white paper]. State College, PA: Fong Strategy.
Kotler, P., & Keller, K. (2011). *Marketing management,* 14th ed. Upper Saddle River, NJ: Pearson.
Noel-Levitz. (2012). *Why did they enroll? The factors influencing college choice.* Retrieved from https://www.noellevitz.com/documents/shared/Papers_and_Research/2012/2012_Factors_to_Enroll.pdf
Pew Research Center. (2012). *Biennial media consumption survey.* Washington, DC: Author.
Trout, J., & Ries, A. (2000). *Positioning: The battle for your mind.* New York, NY: McGraw-Hill.
University Professional and Continuing Education Association (UPCEA). (2006). *Management report.* Washington, DC: Author.
University Professional and Continuing Education Association (UPCEA). (2007). *Management report.* Washington, DC: Author.

University Professional and Continuing Education Association (UPCEA). (2008). *Management report*. Washington, DC: Author.
University Professional and Continuing Education Association (UPCEA). (2009). *Management report*. Washington, DC: Author.
University Professional and Continuing Education Association (UPCEA). (2011a). *Management report*. Washington, DC: Author.
University Professional and Continuing Education Association (UPCEA). (2011b). *Marketing report*. Washington, DC: Author.
University Professional and Continuing Education Association (UPCEA). (2012a). *Client study of social media*. Washington, DC: Author.
University Professional and Continuing Education Association (UPCEA). (2012b). *Proprietary study of an institution's marketing and competitors*. Washington, DC: Author.
University Professional and Continuing Education Association (UPCEA). (2013). *Working paper on customer relationship management*. Washington, DC: Author.

JAMES FONG, MS, MBA, *is the founding director of the University Professional and Continuing Education Association's Center for Research and Consulting.*

8

The aging and longevity of the U.S. population presents challenging opportunities for adult and continuing educators in higher education.

Continuing Higher Education and Older Adults: A Growing Challenge and Golden Opportunity

Frank R. DiSilvestro

Educating older adults has been important to adult and continuing education for years, but the reality of a skyrocketing aging population is now upon us. This reality evokes a sense of urgency for adult and continuing educators in higher education to respond. This chapter provides adult and continuing educators with information about our growing aging population, its challenge to continuing higher education, and the importance of higher education to older adults. It also provides references to selected published resources dealing with older adult learning and factors affecting older adults' participation in higher education. It concludes with three examples of how continuing educators in higher education can successfully meet this challenge.

Aging Population

Never before in the history of the United States have there been so many older adults age 65 and over, and the number is growing dramatically. According to Howden and Meyer (2011):

> Between 2000 and 2010, the population under the age of 18 grew at a rate of 2.6 percent. The growth rate was even slower for those aged 18–44 (0.6 percent). This contrasts with the substantially faster growth rates seen at the older ages. Finally, the population aged 45–64 grew at a rate of 31.5 percent. The population aged 65 and older also grew at a faster rate (15.1 percent) than the population under age 45. (p. 2)

The large growth of older Americans is due primarily to the aging of the baby boomer population (those who were born between 1945 and 1964). The first wave of baby boomers reached retirement age in 2011, and they will constitute the largest segment of the population shift of adults 65 and older in the next 40 years. This group is projected to grow from 40.2 million in 2010 to 72 million in 2030 and a remarkable 88.5 million in 2050, or more than double the 40.2 million in 2010 (Vincent & Velkoff, 2010). This means that in 2050, 1 in 5 persons will be aged 65 or older. Not only are there more older adults, but they are living longer. In 1900, the life expectancy in the United States was 47; however, in 2015, the life expectancy for males will be 76.5 and for females, 81.4 (U.S. Census Bureau, 2012). Many of these older adults may live into their 90s. In addition to the fact that there will be more older adults who are living longer, new discoveries about neurogenesis and brain plasticity have disproven old beliefs about the limits of older adults' capacity to learn and have opened new horizons for older adults to learn new things (Royal Society, 2011).

Challenge to Continuing Higher Education

The challenge this growing aging population presents to continuing higher education was forecast by Daniel Yankelovich (2005), well-known public policy analyst and social science researcher. Yankelovich predicted what higher education would look like in 2015 if it responded to this changing trend of an increasingly aging society by stating:

> To expand its outreach, higher education will want to strengthen existing programs for the growing numbers of adults who wish to add new areas of competence. Colleges have a strong economic incentive to be more creative over the next decade in matching the needs of older adults with more-suitable materials and more-convenient timetables. If they don't seize the opportunity, they risk losing a significant new source of revenue. (para. 13)

Yankelovich (2005) noted that older adults want and seek ways to enrich their lives. He commented that retirement is taking on new meaning; many older adults are not looking to totally withdraw from work but seek new ways of fulfillment. Most seek ways to keep an active healthy lifestyle, which may include career retooling or even new careers or new goals. "As they seek to build bridges to new life opportunities, many turn to higher education" (para. 11).

Yet universities still need to do more to respond to this clarion call. In a report by Lakin, Mullane, and Robinson (2008) for the American Council of Education, a survey of higher education institutions found that "more than 40 percent of institutions responded that they did not identify older adult students for purposes of outreach, programs and services, or financial aid" (p. 12). Lakin (2009) later stated that although colleges and universities have created more programs to meet older adults, "many more institutions must move beyond one-dimensional views of older adults as lifelong learners" (p. 40). Coulter and Mandell (2012) make it clear that adult learners are still not in the picture of first-tier universities. Higher education needs to better grasp the importance of continuing education for older adults.

What Higher Education Means to an Older Adult

Continuing educators can be strong advocates for these growing numbers of older adults and at the same time make their own institutions of higher education aware of this golden opportunity. There are obvious benefits of higher education for older adults. For example, more highly educated adults fill critical job shortages in society, provide a greater tax base, draw less on the health care system, and constitute a large voting bloc who will be advocates for higher education (Lakin et al., 2008).

Yet beyond these reasons, the most important reason is that higher education contributes value and meaning to the older adult's life. Mary Fasano is an example of just what higher education means to an older adult. At age 89, Fasano was the oldest person ever to earn an undergraduate degree from Harvard. In her graduation address, Fasano said:

> My studies were interrupted when I was in the 7th grade, back sometime around World War I. I loved school but I was forced to leave it to care for my family. I was consigned to work in a Rhode Island cotton mill where I labored for many years. I eventually married and raised 5 children, and 20 grandchildren. But all the while I felt inferior to those around me. I knew I was as smart as a college graduate. I knew I was capable of doing a job well. I had proven it by running a successful business for decades that still exists. But I wanted more. I wanted to feel confident when I spoke, and I wanted people to respect my opinions. …
>
> But I am here today—like you are—to prove that it can be done; that the power gained by understanding and appreciating the world around us can be obtained by anyone regardless of social status, personal challenges, or age. That belief is what has motivated me for the last 75 years to get this degree. (Fasano, 1997, para. 7, 9)

Mary Fasano shows that an older adult values additional learning and that with additional learning an older adult can develop a stronger identity and build confidence that helps with the other challenges of aging.

Older Adults and Higher Education Today. Given the increasing number of older adults and the continued need for universities to better respond to this growing aging population, how can adult and continuing educators promote positive change in our universities to meet this challenge? One way is to become informed about past and present information about education for older adults that will provide insight about what works and what obstacles to avoid in helping older adults successfully participate in higher education. For example, Roger Hiemstra (1980), a prolific adult educator and advocate of older adult learning, provided a comprehensive summary of research about guiding and teaching older adults. Following that publication, Wolf and Fisher (1998) edited a very useful sourcebook that provides adult and continuing educators with information about theory and research in educational gerontology along with information about the practice of older adult learning and education.

More recently, Lamb and Brady (2005) studied members of the Osher Research Institute in Portland, Maine. The study investigated the perceived benefits of participation in a peer-governed and -taught elder learning program. The benefits reported were observed in four areas: intellectual stimulation, experiencing a nurturing and supportive community, enhancing self-esteem, and having opportunities for spiritual renewal. These were the factors that "turned on" participants and caused them to return year after year.

An especially useful and more recent project, *Reinvesting in the Third Age: Older Adults and Higher Education*, was conducted by the American Council of Education, resulting in two reports by Lakin, Mullane, and Robinson (2007, 2008). The first report, titled *Framing New Terrain: Older Adults and Higher Education* (Lakin et al., 2007), was a comprehensive review of current research describing the demographics of this older population, why they participate in higher education, and what barriers they confront. The second report, titled *Mapping New Directions: Higher Education for Older Adults* (Lakin et al., 2008), was a follow-up study to address the questions raised by the first study. The *Mapping New Directions* study utilized focus groups of adults ages 55 to 81, conducted a national survey of higher education institutions, and held roundtable discussions of higher education and government leaders.

Why Older Adults Participate in Higher Education. The *Framing New Terrain* report (Lakin et al., 2007) describes numerous research studies that describe why older adults participate in higher education. For example, it cites the Lamb and Brady (2005) study, which reviewed much of the earlier literature on factors that influenced older adults' participation in higher education. The *Framing New Terrain* report presented other studies by Manheimer (2005) and by Lamdin and Fugate (1997) that underscored the importance of intellectual stimulation and, very importantly, the need for social interaction and sense of community for older adults to participate in higher education.

The report also revealed the important role that work played in the lives of these older adults and the importance of higher education in retooling their current job skills or gaining new knowledge and skills in order to continue working, even during the traditional retirement years. These older adults wanted to work either for income, service, or enjoyment. According to the *Framing New Terrain* study (Lakin et al., 2007): "A recent survey of 1,000 adults aged 50–70 found that 66% of the respondents plan to work during the traditional retirement years" (p. 15).

This information presents opportunities for continuing educators to provide courses and training as well as to partner with businesses to train older adults. The *Framing New Terrain* study (Lakin et al., 2007) also reported an increasing numbers of older adults who continue to work and who would like to receive additional education that would allow them to pursue a new career, and for whom getting a degree is not so important. Sarah Lawrence-Lightfoot (2008) underscored this new trend after interviewing men and women in their 50s, 60s, and 70s to learn the new ways people are embracing life to try out new careers that defied traditional norms.

Focus groups from the *Mapping New Directions* study (Lakin et al., 2008) found three primary motivators for older adults returning to school:

1. *Learning to learn* (the joy of learning). Older adults wanted to pursue learning related to improving the quality of their lives and how they can manage aging. For many, continued learning is a rejuvenating experience. Survey results indicated that higher education institutions reported arts and humanities courses the most popular among older adults, with work-related courses, such as business management and entrepreneurship, a close second.
2. *Learning to connect* (meeting new people in their communities). Older adults wanted to meet and engage with others to learn about other cultures and groups outside of their own small familiar communities. They did not want to be isolated. They preferred intergenerational learning where both young and old share and learn from each other.
3. *Learning to work* (advance careers or pursue new careers). Some older adults wanted to pursue second careers different from the careers that provided them income, while many continued to work just to survive in the current economy. Education was seen as very important with respect to these older adult career goals.

Barriers to Older Adults Participating in Higher Education

The Lakin et al. (2008) research also described many barriers to older adults participating in higher education that continuing educators need to be aware of. Demographic barriers include age, with its additional responsibilities such as family and work responsibilities, and time. Their research revealed that "lack of time is one of the most commonly cited barriers to education among older adults" (p. 18). Race and ethnicity were also mentioned because of the generally poorer health, income level, and especially educational level of older minorities. Geography is important because many older adults live in rural areas, which may not be so conducive for supporting higher education as more urban areas. Attitudinal barriers included ageism on college campuses as well as many adults' negative attitudes about returning to school.

Structural barriers, such as finances and a lack of support services, prevent older adults from returning to school. Lack of funding was one of the main reasons why older adults do not return to higher education. For those with limited income, paying for higher education can be a real struggle, and trying to understand financial aid programs can be a real challenge.

Many older adults with little postsecondary experience need support services because often they are unfamiliar with technology and are sometimes anxious and lack confidence. Older adults often need help with prior learning assessment, career counseling, and job placement.

Higher education institutions themselves face barriers in trying to serve older adults including outreach, programming, and funding. For example, under both outreach and programming, the wide range of motivations and needs of older adults make it difficult for higher educational institutions to communicate with and program for older adults (Lakin et al., 2008).

Programs that Do Work for Older Adults Returning to Higher Education

Knowing why older adults participate in higher education, as well as knowing what obstacles they and higher education face, enable continuing educators to develop successful programs to meet the challenge. Following are three models that successfully meet this challenge.

Osher Lifelong Learning Institutes. The Bernard Osher Foundation, headquartered in San Francisco, is one of the most prominent supporters of older adult learning. The foundation seeks to improve quality of life through support for higher education and the arts. In addition, it supports a national lifelong learning network for seasoned adults through the Osher Lifelong Learning Institute National Resource Center at the University of Southern Maine, Portland (University of Southern Maine, n.d.). The Osher Lifelong Learning Institutes (OLLIs) operate on the campuses of 116 institutions of higher education from Maine to Hawaii and Alaska.

An example of an excellent program for older adults is the OLLI at Northwestern University, which recently celebrated 25 years of serving adults over 50 years old at the university's Chicago and Evanston campuses. This noncredit program is designed for the joy of learning. It is organized by the students themselves and is an excellent example of the social features of adult learning that older adults like so much.

The students themselves conceive and develop study groups that emphasize participation and discussion rather than lectures. The director of the program, Judy Mann, was quoted as saying, "We sometimes say, 'people come here not to be taught, but to learn'" ("For the Pure Joy of Learning," 2012, para. 2). Hundreds of older students have returned to education, and they learn about different topics, from English literature to political science and modern art. Mental stimulation, creativity, and camaraderie are essential ingredients of OLLI's offerings. Today the program offers nearly 155 study groups to 800 members and has offered an impressive 3,800 study groups over a 25-year span.

Mini University at Indiana University. Another example of a successful noncredit program for older adults is Mini University at Indiana University in Bloomington (Indiana University Alumni Association, n.d.). A weeklong summer residential learning experience, Mini University sells out each year. This past year, its 42nd year in operation, it had over 500 participants. Participants can choose from nearly 100 noncredit classes and 15 optional evening activities, such as picnics, tours, and films.

An excellent case study of Mini University and its 40-year history was completed in 2011 (Koop, McCollum, McKinney Han, Nicola, & Treff, 2011). The case study surveyed administrators, faculty, and participants from the June 2011 session and identified elements of the program that made it successful. The results of the research indicated that Mini University is very learner friendly and had diverse course offerings. Interestingly, the results found that most of the participants, 56%, had not attended other programs, which indicated that there is a market for retirees and older learners. Participants overwhelmingly agreed that they liked the topics covered and that the courses fulfilled their need for continuous learning. Developing and forming long-term friendships and looking forward to the social aspects of Mini University were reasons why people return year after year.

Bachelor of General Studies Degree at Indiana University. The Bachelor of General Studies (BGS) is particularly appealing to students who are older, who may have full-time jobs or family responsibilities, who need greater freedom in timing and pacing their education, and who need a variety of learning options. It is offered through Indiana University at different campuses and at a distance. The degree has no major; rather, it is an interdisciplinary degree that includes the arts and humanities, social and behavioral sciences, and mathematics and natural sciences. It allows students to develop their own individualized plan of study to meet their unique goals.

A research study to investigate what graduates did with a BGS degree found that the degree allows students to tailor their academic program to their career interests and prepares them to work in a wide variety of occupations (DiSilvestro & Merrill, 2012). The graduates in this study worked in a variety of occupational fields, led by business and management, and followed by administration, education, health care, and social sciences.

The graduates continued their education in diverse areas, particularly business, liberal arts, and education, and they completed advanced degrees at a variety of well-known colleges and universities. The BGS degree clearly serves as a credential for employment and further education.

Summary

Higher education is important to older adults, and older adults are important to higher education. Adult and continuing educators have an important role in helping colleges and universities understand the characteristics, needs, and aspirations of older adults. There is a wide diversity in the needs of older adults, and the reasons they participate in higher education are multifaceted. Yet higher education must chart new pathways for older adults to participate, and continuing education is poised to do this best. Lifelong learning is an important ingredient for aging well. Older adults not only learn for themselves, but they also contribute to their communities and the higher education institutions that help them. The challenge is clear. The opportunity is real. The time to act is now.

References

Coulter, X., & Mandell, A. (2012). Adult higher education: Are we moving in the wrong direction? *Journal of Continuing Higher Education*, 60(1), 40–42.

DiSilvestro, F., & Merrill, H. (2012). Demonstrating the value of lifelong learning through outcomes assessment research. In C. Boden-McGill & K. King (Eds.), *Conversations about adult learning in our complex world* (pp. 271–286). Charlotte, NC: Information Age.

Fasano, M. (1997, June 12). The power of knowledge. *Harvard University Gazette*. Retrieved from http://news.harvard.edu/gazette/1997/06.12/ThePowerofKnowl.html

For the pure joy of learning. (2012, August 1). *Continuum*. Retrieved from http://www.continuum.northwestern.edu/2012/08/for-the-pure-joy-of-learning/

Hiemstra, R. (1980). *Guiding the older adult learner. Information series No. 209, ERIC Clearinghouse for Adult, Career, and Vocational Education*. ERIC Document Reproduction Service No. 193529. Retrieved from http://www-distance.syr.edu/guiding.html

Howden, M., & Meyer, J. A. (2011). *Age and sex composition: 2010 U.S. Census Bureau Report*. Retrieved from http://www.census.gov/prod/cen2010/briefs/c2010br-03.pdf

Indiana University Alumni Association. (n.d.). *Mini University*. Retrieved from http://alumni.indiana.edu/together/mini-university/index.html

Koop, A., McCollum, K., McKinney Han, K., Nicola, C., & Treff, M. (2012). Indiana University's mini university: A model in lifelong learning. *Journal of Teaching and Education*, 1(4), 317–324.

Lakin, M. B. (2009). Forging new identities: Older adults in higher education. *International Journal of Continuing Education and Lifelong Learning*, 2, 33–44.

Lakin, M. B., Mullane, L., & Robinson, S. P. (2007). *Framing new terrain: Older adults and higher education. Reinvesting in the third age: Older adults and higher education—First report.* Washington, DC: American Council on Education.

Lakin, M. B., Mullane, L., & Robinson, S. P. (2008). *Mapping new directions: Higher education for older adults. Reinvesting in the third age: Older adults and higher education—Second report.* Washington, DC: American Council on Education.

Lamb, R., & Brady, E. M. (2005). Participation in lifelong learning institutes: What turns members on? *Educational Gerontology*, 31(3), 207–224.

Lamdin, L., & Fugate, M. (1997). *Elderlearning: New frontier in an aging society*. Washington, DC: American Council on Education.

Lawrence-Lightfoot, S. (2008). *The third chapter: Passion, risk, and adventure in the 25 years after 50*. New York, NY: Farrar, Straus, and Giroux.

Manheimer, R. J. (2005). The older learner's journey to an ageless society: Lifelong learning on the brink of a crisis. *Journal of Transformative Education*, 3(3), 198–220.

Royal Society. (2011, February). *Brain waves module 2: Neuroscience: Implications for education and lifelong learning*. London, England: Author. Retrieved from http://royalsociety.org/uploadedFiles/Royal_Society_Content/policy/publications/2011/4294975733-With-Appendices.pdf

University of Southern Maine. (n.d.). *Osher Lifelong Learning Institute National Resource Center*. Retrieved from http://usm.maine.edu/olli/national/

U.S. Census Bureau. (2012). *Statistical abstract of the United States*. Washington, DC: U.S. Government Printing Office. Retrieved from http://www.census.gov/compendia/statab/cats/births_deaths_marriages_divorces/life_expectancy.html

Vincent, G. K., & Velkoff, V. A. (2010). *The next four decades: The older population in the United States 2010 to 2050*. Washington, DC: U.S. Census Bureau. Retrieved from http://www.census.gov/prod/2010pubs/p25-1138.pdf

Wolf, M. A., & Fisher, J. C. (Eds.). (1998). *New Directions for Adult and Continuing Education: No. 77. Using learning to meet the challenges of older adulthood*. San Francisco, CA: Jossey-Bass.

Yankelovich, D. (2005, November 25). Ferment and change: Higher education in 2015. *Chronicle of Higher Education*. Retrieved from http://chronicle.com/article/Ferment-Change-Higher/14934

FRANK R. DISILVESTRO is associate professor of adult education, program coordinator for the graduate program in adult education, and part-time associate professor of medical education at Indiana University.

The extent to which continuing educators respond to the challenges and opportunities presented in this volume will determine to a large extent their future relevance to their institutions.

The Road Ahead: Challenges and Opportunities

Ronald G. White

Adult enrollments in both credit and noncredit programs have exploded since the 1980s in response to the need for degree completion, career advancement, and lifelong learning. Despite this growth, this time period also has been characterized by fiscal strains in higher education that have reduced the size of many continuing education (CE) units, eliminated others entirely, and forced more stringent business practices on those that have survived. In addition, the rapid development of new learning technologies has altered the typical CE unit in fundamental ways, and the need for highly trained computer personnel, hardware, and software has had major budgetary impacts.

Continuing educators also have been forced to improve their business acumen in response to an increased emphasis on profit and generating revenue for the larger institution, resulting in increased emphasis on marketing as well as more entrepreneurial programs and outreach. In addition to the traditional program development staff, CE units now hire marketing experts and accountants to measure the impact of marketing campaigns, track demographic and external trends, and chart profits and losses among programs. As a result, there are fewer community service programs and more that generate profits. These expectations demand fundamentally different skills from those previously required of CE personnel.

Smaller budgets, reduced staff, pressures to produce a profit, and more complex and diversified program portfolios now characterize many CE units. It is clearly a time for doing more with less, with a creative and entrepreneurial bent. A number of related trends and issues have been presented in this volume. The ways that we as CE professionals respond to them will determine not only the quality of programs we provide for adult students but the future, and possibly very existence, of our CE schools and divisions.

Additional Options for Adults Seeking Degrees

Although adult degree program enrollment has increased steadily in the past several decades in the United States, the number of adults who actually complete degrees remains stagnant. Baccalaureate degree attainment in the United States lags behind that of many other countries, and efforts have been launched to put the nation back on top in percentage of adults with degrees. These efforts include President Obama's 2020 Initiative (Gast, Chapter 2 of this volume). Private foundations, such as Lumina, also seek to dramatically increase adult graduation rates, and others, like the Bernard Osher Foundation's Osher Reentry Scholars program, provide financial assistance earmarked specifically to older students.

Although most adult students still prefer to attend classes at brick-and-mortar campuses, an increasing number is choosing online study or a hybrid campus/online combination. Online degree and degree completion programs are offered by public, private, and, increasingly, for-profit schools. This last group often faces questions about quality and acceptance of their degrees. For-profits generally do not adhere to the rigorous accreditation standards of traditional public and private institutions; because they have their own accreditation agencies, comparisons of outcomes are sometimes difficult.

Renewed efforts to reduce barriers to participation in higher education are taking place. These efforts address cost and financial aid, lack of readily available and accessible information, competing pressures of adult life, and transfer credit policies that make it difficult to apply credits earned earlier—sometimes decades earlier. The need for support services geared for adult learners remains as strong as when many of these programs began as centers for women returning to school in the 1970s and 1980s.

Increased Focus on Strategic Partnerships

Higher education institutions are increasingly partnering with external organizations for multiple reasons, including the blurring of the line between school and work, which requires that workers continuously upgrade skills to remain competitive. Other partnerships with industry help to underwrite the expense of research as well as scientific, medical, and computer technology in a time of reduced academic budgets. Other partnerships connect secondary education, community colleges, and baccalaureate-granting institutions to articulate curricula, facilitate more seamless transition, and improve retention.

The fact that CE units have experience partnering with external groups, such as government agencies and employers, as well as with academic departments, should place them in a pivotal role in developing partnerships of all kinds. Partnerships with academic departments to develop educational and training programs for external clients are increasingly important to the bottom line of CE as well as to its mission to extend the resources of the campus into the community (often employing alternative delivery methods).

Since the culture of the typical CE unit is more entrepreneurial and quicker to respond than that of traditional academic departments, it is critical that expectations, roles, and fiscal arrangements be clearly understood before a program jointly sponsored with an academic department begins.

Greater Use of Technology

Arguably the biggest development in CE in recent decades is the advent of online learning, the latest form of distance education. CE units, of course, have a long history of providing learning opportunities to students at a distance, going back a century to the beginnings of correspondence study and agricultural extension. Thus, it is not surprising that CE units have played a major role in the evolution of online learning. Providers include universities, community colleges, and a growing number of for-profit schools; spend one hour watching television and you'll be exposed to multiple ads for (mostly) for-profit providers.

Many online programs started in CE units but have since migrated to "regular" academic departments, sometimes in partnership with CE. A common model is for the academic department to provide instruction and curriculum while CE provides marketing and registration, technical support, fiscal management, and overall administration. Some CE units also assist with instructor orientation and the provision of student support services at a distance. Given the wide range of online programs available, the customer-oriented focus of most CE units can be a major contributor to success, especially when partnering with academic departments where this mind-set is not typically so common.

The latest development in online learning is massive open online courses, or MOOCs. MOOCs are free, open-enrollment courses, often taught by top faculty at prestigious universities. The impact of MOOCs cuts across multiple topics in this issue to include degree and noncredit programs, prior learning assessment, and technology.

Assessing Learning Outside the Classroom

Prior learning assessment (PLA) has been part of the adult education landscape for decades. Learning that has occurred outside of the classroom, whether on the job, through corporate training or military service, volunteer activities, or self-study, is assessed through exams, portfolios, and faculty review of courses and training programs.

Recently there has been a surge in interest in PLA, largely as a result of the renewed focus on degree completion as well as greater awareness of the links between education and the workplace. Not only does PLA provide means to earn college credit beyond seat time for adults, but studies show that students are much more likely to complete degree studies if PLA is incorporated.

New technologies also provide additional means for adults to learn and acquire competencies—YouTube lectures, Apple's iTunes University, badges, and MOOCs provide a wealth of self-study opportunities. In addition, an emerging emphasis on competence-based degree programs, as opposed to merely accumulating credit hours, also has contributed to greater interest in PLA.

Trends Affecting Noncredit Programming

The same societal and technological changes affecting all of higher education have had a particular impact on the noncredit programming in CE units. The need to constantly upgrade career competencies, develop basic academic skills, maintain licensure and certification, and foster lifelong learning for growing numbers of elders inform the noncredit offerings of many CE units. Many programs have changed from community service to a more entrepreneurial focus in response to learner demand and institutional fiscal expectations. Online delivery has broadened the service area of many CE units from local or regional to national and even international.

Both credit and noncredit certificate programs have proliferated in response to the demand for career skills, as have contractual training programs for employers. The range of noncredit programming has also grown to encompass precollege programs to senior citizens. Even the distinction between credit and noncredit programs is beginning to blur as MOOCs and certificate programs attract growing numbers of adults who seek credentials for advancement.

Increased Participation in Economic Development

Increasingly, CE providers are being asked to participate in the development of programs to promote local and statewide economic development, especially those in state-funded universities. Due to their missions and greater connections with their locales, community colleges, in particular, are forging alliances with private industry and local government planning agencies to upgrade skills and enhance competitiveness. Government-sponsored training grants to attract and retain companies often fund these efforts, although some are offered on a contract or tuition basis. A wide variety of skills is taught, ranging from management, computer technology, advanced manufacturing, to soft skills. Additionally, community colleges provide business incubators, networking sessions, coaching, and mentoring.

Growing Numbers of Older Adults

The cohort of adults 65 and older has never been larger in American history, due largely to the maturation of the postwar baby boom generation as well as increased longevity. A larger percentage of "boomers" have college educations than do earlier generations, making it more likely that they will continue to engage in learning throughout their lives.

Recent advances in aging research have demonstrated that older adults' capacity to learn remains strong. This finding presents opportunities for CE programs to provide career skills for those who seek to work at least part-time in retirement as well as programs for those who wish to engage in lifelong learning for personal growth and enjoyment.

To attract these older learners, higher education will have to adapt curricula, instructional approaches, and support services for this audience.

Financial aid, prior learning assessment, outreach, and counseling will need to increase as well. Both community colleges and universities are reaching out to this mature audience, some with program models funded by groups like the Bernard Osher Foundation's Lifelong Learning Institutes, which support older adult lifelong learning in all 50 states.

Program Promotion in an Online World

A revolution has taken place in marketing CE programs. Just a few decades ago, the word *marketing* was seldom heard in universities, a vestige of the private sector that was supposedly beneath lofty institutions of higher education. Today, marketing is an integral function of CE units, with new technologies that have altered the ways that programs are promoted. Marketing professionals need to increase their skills dramatically to encompass new concepts such as strategic marketing, e-marketing, social media marketing, and customer relations management. In addition, reduced budgets require a renewed focus on marketing metrics and measures of effectiveness.

Prior to the late 1990s, marketing staff typically included writers, designers, editors, public relations experts, and production personnel. Today, sophisticated data analysis, and knowledge of social media, the Internet, and new instructional technologies must inform the marketing professional.

Final Thoughts

To meet the challenges and changes that are occurring in higher education and specifically in CE units, there should be greater cooperation with other units of the university. CE also should align its mission with that of the larger institution.

The nurturing of both internal and external relationships will become even more vital to the success of CE units. Faculty and community advisory committees are a good means of beginning to move in this direction. Also, alumni constitute a potential audience—already presumably with some loyalty to the institution—that would allow CE units to work with academic departments to respond to the CE needs of degree holders.

A well-thought-out strategic planning process that also incorporates internal and external groups helps to develop and cement partnering arrangements.

CE units possess skills that are increasingly needed in the rest of academe today, even if they are not immediately recognized or valued. With careful planning and outreach, CE units can position themselves at the very core of their institutional missions, a good thing for the unit, the larger institution, and, most important, our adult students.

RONALD G. WHITE, *EdD, is adjunct associate professor of adult education at Indiana University, where he also served as executive director of continuing studies for the Bloomington campus.*

Index

Abu Dhabi (United Arab Emirates), 11
Academic departments, partnerships with: benefits continuing education unit brings to, 30–32; building successful, 35–36; and contract and intellectual property expertise, 31; and contractual arrangements, 32–33; defining, 28–30; and difficulty with communication, 35; and dissatisfaction with partnership, 35; financial arrangements in, 33–34; and financial expertise, 31–32; and financial reporting, 33; and funding faculty, 34; and market research expertise, 30; and marketing expertise, 31; and policy expertise, 32; and reducing financial risk, 33–34; and registration expertise, 31; and technology expertise, 30–31; and unsuitability for partnership, 34
Acme Industries (Elk Grove Village, Illinois), 74
Adult Degree Programs: additional options in, 102; and adult student support services, 22–23; and best practices, 23; current trends in, 17–24; and enrollment trends among adult students, 18; future considerations for, 24; and hybrid degree programs, 19–20; and issue of transfer credits, 20–21; and massive open online courses (MOOCs), 20; and online degree programs, 18; perceived barriers to, 18–19; and prior learning assessments (PLAs), 20–21; response of public universities to trends in, 19–20; and specialized services, 22–23
Alfred P. Sloan Foundation, 39
Allen, H. A., 47
Allen, I. E., 7–10
Allen, N. H., 28
American Association of Community Colleges (AACC), 76
American Council on Education, 3, 20
American Recovery and Reinvestment Act of 2009 (ARRA), 12, 69
Arkansas Department of Workforce Services, 72
Arkansas Tech University, Ozark Campus (ATU-Ozark Campus), 72
Arsenal of Innovation (Michigan Economic Development Council), 73
Ashcroft, J. C., 4, 39
Aslanian, G., 7, 14
Association of Continuing Education, 9
AT&T, 47
Audant, B., 76
Auto Communities Consortium, 74

Baden, C., 1
Bailey, T. M., 18
Baker, N. C., 4, 61, 66
Bernard Osher Foundation, 62, 84, 104; Osher Reentry Scholars, 102
Biden, Joe, 69
Biden, Jill, 69
Bill & Melinda Gates Foundation, 20
Blair, A., 72
Blondin, J., 72
Boeck, D., 29
Borbely, E., 66
Bowling Green State University, 40; Academic Charter, 40
Bradley, H., 71
Brady, E. M., 82
Braverman, L. R., 4, 7, 13
BRIC (Brazil, Russia, India, and China) nations, 12
Brigham Young University, 42
Brooklyn Economic Development Council, 76

CAEL. *See* Council for Adult Experiential Learning (CAEL)
California State University, Office of Extended and Continuing Education, 12–13
Carnegie Mellon University, 11
Cervero, R., 1
Chen, J., 55
Christensen, C. M., 43
"Collaboration and Partnership: Our Keys to the Future" (Association of Continuing Higher Education), 9
College Foundation, 13
College Level Examination Program (CLEP), 21–22
Committee on Institutional Cooperation, 19

107

Community college, role of, in economic development: and Arkansas Partnership, 72; entrepreneurship and, 75–76; and Harper College, 74–75; and Ivy Tech Community College, 75; and Kingsborough Community College, 76; and Macomb Community College, 73–74; and special challenges of rural colleges, 76–77; and Virtual Incubation Network (VIN), 76; and White Mountains Community College, 77; and workforce training or economic development, 71–72

Continuing Education Review (CHER), 42

Continuing higher education: and better business, 8–9; and corporate education and outreach, 13; and demographic shifts, 13–14; and distance education, 10–11; and innovation, 9–10; international partnerships in, 11–12; programs that work for, 84–85; redefining new roles, responsibilities, and expectations of, 7–14; and workforce education and training, 12–13

Continuing higher education, older adults and, 77–86; and aging population, 79–80, 104–105; and Bachelor of General Studies Degree at Indiana University, 85; barriers to, 83–84; and challenge to continuing higher education, 79–80; and Mini University at Indiana University, 85; and Osher Lifelong Learning Institutes, 84–85; and what higher education means to older adults, 81–83

Continuing higher education, strategic marketing challenges for, 89–99; and branding and strategic positioning, 95–96; and developing marketer, 98–99; introduction to, 89–91; and marketing professional development interests, 93; and new media, 97–98; and number of specific marketing staff by size, 95; organizational structure for, 91–95; and percentage of marketing departments with specific employees by size of department, 94; rating of marketers by deans and marketing leaders, 91; role of information in, 96–97

Conway, M., 72
Coons, M., 74
Coulter, X., 81
Council for Adult Experiential Learning (CAEL), 21, 51, 53–55, 57, 58; Learning Counts program, 22, 54–55

Coursera, 47
Customized training, 71

DANTES Subject Standardization Tests (DSST), 21–22
DiSilvestro, F. R., 4, 79, 85
Distance education (DE), 39, 40
Distance education (DE), from access to excess in: and anticipation, 45; and continuous change, 43; and flexibility, 45–46; and funding balance, 46–47; and institutional acceptance, 45; and institutional cooperation, 41; introduction to, 39–40; and peer review, 42; and profit, 43–44; and quality standards, 41–42; and research, 42–43; three forces of, 40

DIY U: Edupunks, Edupreneurs and the Coming Transformation of Higher Education (Kamenetz), 47

Do It Yourself University (Kamenetz), 47
Duke University, 20
Dundar, A., 55
Dyer, J., 77

Economic participation, increased participation in, 104
Economist, 10
Eduventures, 18
eMarketer, 93
English, A. M., 4, 27

Facebook, 11, 98
Fain, P., 18, 24
Fasano, M., 81
Fiddler, M., 57
Fisher, J. C., 82
Flannery, M. E., 69
Florida Degree Completion Pilot Project, 46
Florida Senate Web site, 46
Fong, J., 4, 89–91, 95, 97
"For the Pure Joy of Learning" (Mann), 84
Framing New Terrain: Older Adults and Higher Education (Lakin, Mullane, and Robinson), 82
Friedman, T., 3, 13
Fugate, M., 82

Garland, J. C., 44
Garrison, D. R., 41
Gast, A., 4, 17, 102
Georgia Tech, 45, 47
Goal 2020 (Obama), 17

Goal 2025 (Lumina Foundation), 17, 47
Grad TX consortium, 21
Gratton, L., 2
Great Brain Race: How Global Universities are Reshaping the World (Wildavsky), 11
Great Depression, 12
Great Recession (2008), 8
Green Bay Packaging, 72, 73; Arkansas Kraft Division, 73
Green Giles, N., 7

Hancock Shaker Village, 31
Handbook of Adult and Continuing Education (Hatfield), 40
Harper College (Palatine, Illinois), 74
Harvard University, 3, 20, 35–36, 45, 81; Division of Continuing Education (DCE), 31; Extension School, 31
HASTAC (Humanities, Arts, Science, and Technology Advanced Collaboratory), 55–56
Hatfield, T. M., 40
Health Care and Education Reconciliation Act (2010), 69
Heller, N., 28
Helmer, M., 72
Hiemstra, R., 82
Hobsons (education solutions company), 97
Horn, M. B., 43
Hossler, D., 55
Howden, M., 79
Hussar, W. J., 18

IACEE. *See* International Association for Continuing Engineering Education
Indiana University, Bloomington, 85; Bachelor of General Studies Degree (BGS), 85; Mini University, 85
Indiana University IU Online, 19
Integrated Post-Secondary Data Education System (IPEDS), 45
Inter Organizational Task Force on Online Learning, 39
International Association for Continuing Engineering Education (IACEE), 66
Iowa Admissions Partnership Program, 21
Iowa State University, 21
iTunes University (iTunesU), 53, 103
Ivy Tech Community College (Indiana), 75

Jacobs, J., 74
Jaschik, S., 12

John D. and Catherine T. MacArthur Foundation, 55–56
Johns Hopkins University, 12
Johnson, C. W., 43

Kamenetz, A., 47
Kansas State University (KSU), 20, 21
Kant, I., 40
Kasworm, C., 2
Keller, K., 96
Kelly, P. J., 17
Kingsborough Community College (New York), 76
Klein-Collins, R., 4, 51–54
Kohl, K. J., 18
Koop, A., 85
Kotler, P., 96
Kroger, 75

Laitinen, A., 54
Lakin, M. B., 81–84
Lamb, R., 82
Lamdin, L., 82
Lapiner, R. S., 13, 63
Laserna, C., 31, 35–36
Lawrence-Lightfoot, S., 83
Learning, assessing, outside classroom, 103
Lederman, D., 54
LEDOs (local economic development organizations), 69, 70
Leitner, H., 31, 35–36
Lewin, T., 3
LinkedIn, 11, 98
Long Island University, 14
Lumina Foundation, 17, 47, 53, 54; Degree Qualifications Profile, 54; Goal 2025, 17, 27, 47

Macomb Community College (Warren, Michigan), 73–74; Learning Unit, 73
Mandell, A., 81
Manheimer, R. J., 82
Mann, J., 84
Manufacturing Skills Standards Council (MSSC), 74
Mapping New Directions: Higher Education for Older Adults (Lakin, Mullane, and Robinson), 82
Marienau, C., 57
Marklein, M. B., 20
Massachusetts Institute of Technology (MIT), 3, 20, 44, 45

McClure, W. S., 31, 35
McCollum, K., 85
McKinney Han, K., 85
Merrill, H., 85
Meyer, J. A., 79
Michigan Economic Development Council Corporation, 73
Michigan State University, 20
Miller, M. R., 31, 35
Mogilyanskaya, A., 20
Monster.com, 71
MOOCs (massive open online courses), 3, 4, 10, 20, 28, 46, 53, 54, 57, 62, 65, 66, 103
Moroney, P., 29
Morrill Act (1862), 40
Morrilton, Arkansas, 72
Mozilla Foundation and Peer 2 Peer University, 3, 55–56
Mullane, L., 81–84
Mullin, C. M., 8

Nation Pizza and Foods (Schaumburg, Illinois), 74
National Center for Education Statistics, 7, 14, 18
National Commission on Higher Education Attainment, 45, 52
National Emergency Act, 12
National Student Clearinghouse Research Center, 55
National University Extension Association Records, 42
Navistar, 75
New and Aspiring Leaders program (UCPEA), 9
New Economy Initiative (Michigan), 73
New York Times, 3
New York University (NYU), 11
Nickoli, R. A., 4, 69
Nicola, C., 85
No Significant Difference Phenomenon (Russell), 42
Noel-Levitz, 18, 19, 92
Noncredit programs: future trends in, 66–67; and multiple stakeholders for CE programs, 62–64; program considerations for, 64–66; trends and considerations affecting, 61–67, 104
Northern Forest Lands Council 10th Anniversary Forum, 77
Northern Forest Sustainable Economy Initiative (SEI), 77
Northwestern University, 84
"Not What It Used to Be" (*Economist*), 10

Obama, B., 17, 52, 102
OER (open and free educational resources), 53
Ohio State University, 8
OLLIs. *See* Osher Lifelong Learning Institutes (OLLIs)
Online world, program promotion in, 105
Open Badges project (Mozilla), 3, 55–56
Open textbooks, 53
Osher Lifelong Learning Institute, National Resource Center (University of Southern Maine), 82, 84
Osher Lifelong Learning Institutes (OLLIs), 28, 62, 84–85

Palmer, I., 53
Peale, C., 3
Peer 2 Peer University, 56
Pennsylvania State University, 23, 42
Perdana University (Malaysia), 12
Pew Research Center, 98
Phillippe, K., 8
PLA. *See* Prior learning assessment (PLA)
Princeton University, 45
Prior learning assessment (PLA): and adult degree programs, 20–21; and assessing learning outside classroom, 103; background to, 52–53; and badges or microcredentials, 55–56; and competency-based degree programs, 54–55; and DIY learning option: OER and MOOCs, 53–54; and faculty support, 57–58; and financial aid, 58; growing importance of, 51–58; and student mobility and credit transfer, 55; vision of expanded uses for, 53–57; and worker-to-worker connection, 56–57; and workforce development, 56
Procurement Technical Assistance Centers (PTACS), 73
Program Integrity Rules (U.S. Department of Education), 44
PTACS. *See* Procurement Technical Assistance Centers (PTACS)
Pure Power Technology (PPT), 75

Quality Matters, 45

Reinvesting in the Third Age: Older Adults and Higher Education (American Council of Education), 82
Ries, A., 96
Robinson, S. P., 81–84

Royal Society, 80
Russell, T. L., 42

Salesforce, 97
Sams, G., 73
San Jose State University (SJSU), 40, 46–47
Saving Alma Mater: A Rescue Plan for America's Public Universities (Garland), 44
Sawyer, J., 73–74
Scalzo, K., 66
Schroeder, R., 3, 39
Seaman, J., 7–10
Shapiro, D., 55
Sherman, A., 53
Simonson, M., 40
Singapore, 11
Sloan Consortium, 7–10
Small Business Development Council, 76
Smith, P., 44
Smith, S. G., 75
Southern Michigan Community College Consortium, 73–74
Southern New Hampshire (SNHU) Communications Office, 45
Special Collections Research Center, 42
Stamats Higher Education Marketing, 10–11
Stanford Artificial Intelligence Laboratory, 46
Stanford University, 3, 45
State University of New York (SUNY), 8
Strategic partnerships, increased focus on, 102–103
Stratford, M., 19
SunGard, 97
SUNY Farmingdale State College, 13
Suresh, S., 11
Syracuse University Library, 42

Taylor, M. C., 41
Technology, greater use for, 103
Texas Tech University, 42
Thrun, S., 46, 47
Tilghman, C., 28, 47
Tisch Asia (New York University), 11
Title IV funding, 58, 75
Torres, V., 55
Trade Act (1974), 69
Trade Adjustment Assistance Community College and Career Training (TAACCT), 12
Treff, M., 85
Trout, J., 96
Twitter, 11, 98

Udacity, 46, 47
United Auto Workers (UAW), 75
United States Distance Learning Association, 40
University Continuing Education Association, 61
University of California, Berkeley, 42, 45
University of California, Los Angeles (UCLA), 13
University of Florida, 42
University of Illinois, Springfield, 39
University of Indiana, Bloomington, Adult Student Resources, 23
University of Maryland, 8
University of Massachusetts, Amherst, 31, 35
University of Missouri, Columbia, 42
University of Nebraska, Lincoln, 20, 42; Online, 19
University of South Carolina (USC): Palmetto College, 19–20
University of Southern Maine, Portland, 84
University of Texas, Austin, 42
University of Washington, 45; Professional and Continuing Education, 29–32, 34, 35
University of Wisconsin, Madison, 23
University of Wisconsin e-Campus, 19, 45
University Professional Continuing Education Association (UPCEA), 8–10, 39, 42, 61, 89–98; Center for Research and Consulting (CRC), 89–90; Independent Study Division, 42; Professional, Continuing, and Online Education Update, 45
University System of Georgia, 63, 65
UPCEA. *See* University Professional Continuing Education Association (UPCEA)
U.S. Census Bureau, 80
U.S. Department of Education, 17, 44–46
U.S. Department of Labor, 9, 12, 52, 69, 74; Trade Adjustment Assistance Community College and Career Training Grant Program, 52; Training and Employment Guidance Letter 15-10, 52, 56

Velkoff, V. A., 80
VIN. *See* Virtual Incubation Network (VIN)
Vincent, G. K., 80
Virtual Incubation Network (VIN), 76

Walshok, M., 2, 62
Warden, K., 72
Watters, A., 3
Wertheim, J. B., 4, 51
Western Association of Schools and Colleges, 24
Western Interstate Commission for Higher Education (WICHE), 17, 20, 22, 42; Cooperative for Educational Technologies (WCET), 42
Whitaker, R., 28, 47
Whitaker, U., 57
White, R. G., 4, 101
White Mountains Community College (New Hampshire), 77

WICHE. *See* Western Interstate Commission for Higher Education (WICHE)
Wildavsky, B., 11
Wolf, M. A., 82
Wolfgang, B., 19
Workforce Investment Boards (WIBs), 12
Wyatt, L. G., 22, 23

Yale University, 11
Yankelovich, D., 1, 2, 80
YouTube, 53, 66, 98, 103

Zerquera, D., 55
Ziskin, M., 55

Great Resources for Higher Education Professionals

Student Affairs Today
12 issues for $225 (print) / $180 (e)

Get innovative best practices for student affairs plus lawsuit summaries to keep your institution out of legal trouble. It's packed with advice on offering effective services, assessing and funding programs, and meeting legal requirements.
studentaffairstodaynewsletter.com

Campus Legal Advisor
12 issues for $210 (print) / $170 (e)

From complying with the ADA and keeping residence halls safe to protecting the privacy of student information, this monthly publication delivers proven strategies to address the tough legal issues you face on campus.
campuslegaladvisor.com

Campus Security Report
12 issues for $210 (print) / $170 (e)

A publication that helps you effectively manage the challenges in keeping your campus, students, and employees safe. From protecting students on campus after dark to interpreting the latest laws and regulations, *Campus Security Report* has answers you need.
campussecurityreport.com

National Teaching & Learning Forum
6 issues for $65 (print or e)

From big concepts to practical details and from cutting-edge techniques to established wisdom, NTLF is your resource for cross-disciplinary discourse on student learning. With it, you'll gain insights into learning theory, classroom management, lesson planning, scholarly publishing, team teaching, online learning, pedagogical innovation, technology, and more.
ntlf.com

Disability Compliance for Higher Education
12 issues for $230 (print) / $185 (e)

This publication combines interpretation of disability laws with practical implementation strategies to help you accommodate students and staff with disabilities. It offers data collection strategies, intervention models for difficult students, service review techniques, and more.
disabilitycomplianceforhighereducation.com

Dean & Provost
12 issues for $225 (print) / $180 (e)

From budgeting to faculty tenure and from distance learning to labor relations, *Dean & Provost* gives you innovative ways to manage the challenges of leading your institution. Learn how to best use limited resources, safeguard your institution from frivolous lawsuits, and more.
deanandprovost.com

Enrollment Management Report
12 issues for $230 (print) / $185 (e)

Find out which enrollment strategies are working for your colleagues, which aren't, and why. This publication gives you practical guidance on all aspects—including records, registration, recruitment, orientation, admissions, retention, and more.
enrollmentmanagementreport.com

WANT TO SUBSCRIBE?
Go online or call: 888.378.2537.

JOSSEY-BASS
A Wiley Brand

Great Resources for Higher Education Professionals

College Athletics and the Law
12 issues for $225 (print) / $180 (e)

Develop a legally sound "game plan" for your institution's athletic programs! Each month, you get expert coaching on how to meet NCAA and Title IX requirements, negotiate coaching contracts, support athletes with disabilities, and more.
collegeathleticslaw.com

FERPA Answer Book and Bulletin
6 issues for $220 (print only)

Includes a full binder with all you need to know about FERPA
From safekeeping students' education records to learning how you can share personal information, this is your professional survival guide. It includes the latest changes to the regs, how to comply, and newly issued FPCO policy letters, administrative and judicial decisions, and more.

About Campus
6 issues for $65 (print only)

An exciting and eclectic mix of articles — designed to illuminate the critical issues faced by both student affairs and academic affairs as they work on their shared goal: to help students learn. Topics include promoting student learning, meeting the needs of a diverse student population, assessing student learning, and accommodating the changing student culture.

Assessment Update
6 issues for $135 (print) / $110 (e)

Get the latest assessment techniques for higher education. *Assessment Update* is your resource for evaluating learning communities, performance indicators, assessing student engagement, using electronic portfolios, new assessment approaches and more.
assessmentupdate.com

Recruiting & Retaining Adult Learners
12 issues for $225 (print) / $180 (e)

This publication addresses the challenges and opportunities you face in recruiting, retaining, and educating your adult students. Find strategies to target your orientation to adult learners, encourage adult-friendly support systems, take advantage of new technologies, and more.
recruitingretainingadultlearners.com

The Successful Registrar
12 issues for $230 (print) / $185 (e)

Get practical guidance on all aspects of your job—from implementing the newest technology and successful registration programs to complying with FERPA, and from training your staff and student workers to security issues and transcript management.
thesuccessfulregistrar.com

The Department Chair
4 issues for $99 (print) / $89 (e)

From retaining your best faculty and resolving conflict to measuring learning and implementing new policies, this resource arms you with the practical information you need to manage your department effectively.
departmentchairs.org/journal.aspx

WANT TO SUBSCRIBE?
Go online or call: 888.378.2537.

JOSSEY-BASS
A Wiley Brand

Statement of Ownership

Statement of Ownership, Management, and Circulation (required by 39 U.S.C. 3685), filed on OCTOBER 1, 2013 for NEW DIRECTIONS FOR ADULT AND CONTINUING EDUCATION (Publication No. 1052-2891), published Quarterly for an annual subscription price of $89 at Wiley Subscription Services, Inc., at Jossey-Bass, One Montgomery St., Suite 1200, San Francisco, CA 94104-4594.

The names and complete mailing addresses of the Publisher, Editor, and Managing Editor are: Publisher, Wiley Subscription Services, Inc., A Wiley Company at San Francisco, One Montgomery St., Suite 1200, San Francisco, CA 94104-4594; Editor, Co-Editor - Susan Imel, 3076 Woodbine Place, Columbus, OH 43202-1341; Managing Editor, Co-Editor- Jovita M. Ross-Gordon, Texas State University, CLAS Dept. 601 University Dr., San Marcos, TX 78666. Contact Person: Joe Schuman; Telephone: 415-782-3232.

NEW DIRECTIONS FOR ADULT AND CONTINUING EDUCATION is a publication owned by Wiley Subscription Services, Inc., 111 River St., Hoboken, NJ 07030. The known bondholders, mortgagees, and other security holders owning or holding 1% or more of total amount of bonds, mortgages, or other securities are(see list).

	Average No. Copies Each Issue During Preceding 12 Months	No. Copies Of Single Issue Published Nearest To Filing Date (Summer 2013)
15a. Total number of copies (net press run)	743	570
15b. Legitimate paid and/or requested distribution (by mail and outside mail)		
15b(1). Individual paid/requested mail subscriptions stated on PS form 3541 (include direct written request from recipient, telemarketing, and Internet requests from recipient, paid subscriptions including nominal rate subscriptions, advertiser's proof copies, and exchange copies)	221	209
15b(2). Copies requested by employers for distribution to employees by name or position, stated on PS form 3541	0	0
15b(3). Sales through dealers and carriers, street vendors, counter sales, and other paid or requested distribution outside USPS	0	0
15b(4). Requested copies distributed by other mail classes through USPS	0	0
15c. Total paid and/or requested circulation (sum of 15b(1), (2), (3), and (4))	221	209
15d. Nonrequested distribution (by mail and outside mail)		
15d(1). Outside county nonrequested copies stated on PS form 3541	52	51

	Average No. Copies Each Issue During Preceding 12 Months	No. Copies Of Single Issue Published Nearest To Filing Date (Summer 2013)
15d(2). In-county nonrequested copies stated on PS form 3541	0	0
15d(3). Nonrequested copies distributed through the USPS by other classes of mail	0	0
15d(4). Nonrequested copies distributed outside the mail	52	51
15e. Total nonrequested distribution (sum of 15d(1), (2), (3), and (4))	273	260
15f. Total distribution (sum of 15c and 15e)	470	310
15g. Copies not distributed	0	0
15h. Total (sum of 15f and 15g)	743	570
15i. Percent paid and/or requested circulation (15c divided by 15f times 100)	81.2%	80.3%

I certify that all information furnished on this form is true and complete. I understand that anyone who furnishes false or misleading information on this form or who omits material or information requested on this form may be subject to criminal sanctions (including fines and imprisonment) and/or civil sanctions (including civil penalties).

Statement of Ownership will be printed in the Winter 2013 issue of this publication.

(signed) Susan E. Lewis, VP & Publisher-Periodicals

NEW DIRECTIONS FOR ADULT AND CONTINUING EDUCATION
ORDER FORM SUBSCRIPTION AND SINGLE ISSUES

DISCOUNTED BACK ISSUES:

Use this form to receive 20% off all back issues of *New Directions for Adult and Continuing Education*. All single issues priced at **$23.20** (normally $29.00).

TITLE	ISSUE NO.	ISBN
_____	_____	_____
_____	_____	_____

Call 888-378-2537 or see mailing instructions below. When calling, mention the promotional code JBNND to receive your discount. For a complete list of issues, please visit www.josseybass.com/go/ndace

SUBSCRIPTIONS: (1 YEAR, 4 ISSUES)

☐ New Order ☐ Renewal

U.S.	☐ Individual: $89	☐ Institutional: $311
CANADA/MEXICO	☐ Individual: $89	☐ Institutional: $351
ALL OTHERS	☐ Individual: $113	☐ Institutional: $385

Call 888-378-2537 or see mailing and pricing instructions below.
Online subscriptions are available at www.onlinelibrary.wiley.com

ORDER TOTALS:

Issue / Subscription Amount: $ _____
Shipping Amount: $ _____
(for single issues only – subscription prices include shipping)
Total Amount: $ _____

SHIPPING CHARGES:
First Item $6.00
Each Add'l Item $2.00

(No sales tax for U.S. subscriptions. Canadian residents, add GST for subscription orders. Individual rate subscriptions must be paid by personal check or credit card. Individual rate subscriptions may not be resold as library copies.)

BILLING & SHIPPING INFORMATION:

☐ **PAYMENT ENCLOSED:** *(U.S. check or money order only. All payments must be in U.S. dollars.)*

☐ **CREDIT CARD:**   ☐ VISA   ☐ MC   ☐ AMEX

Card number _____ Exp. Date _____
Card Holder Name _____ Card Issue # _____
Signature _____ Day Phone _____

☐ **BILL ME:** *(U.S. institutional orders only. Purchase order required.)*

Purchase order # _____
Federal Tax ID 13559302 • GST 89102-8052

Name _____
Address _____
Phone _____ E-mail _____

Copy or detach page and send to: **John Wiley & Sons, One Montgomery Street, Suite 1200, San Francisco, CA 94104-4594**

Order Form can also be faxed to: **888-481-2665**

PROMO JBNND

CPSIA information can be obtained
at www.ICGtesting.com
Printed in the USA
FSHW021612061218
54286FS